Feng Shui

Demystified

II

A Comprehensive Course On
Flying Star Feng Shui And
Famous Water Formulae

by

ULRICH WILHELM LIPPELT

First published by AuthorHouse 09/23/04

ISBN: 1-4184-6381-7 (e-book)
ISBN: 1-4184-3176-1 (Paperback)

Library of Congress Control Number: 2004092137

Printed in the United States of America
Bloomington, IN

This book is printed on acid free paper.

Table of Contents

Introduction

Feng Shui is not to be believed, but to be understood.

The different concepts of traditional schools of Chinese Feng Shui may confuse the student of this ancient method of harmonizing nature's energies for the benefit of mankind.

Many of the Feng Shui practitioners uphold and apply the concepts of their school's masters and disregard the differing teachings of others. All traditional schools possess a rich treasure of experiences collected and preserved by innumerable generations of practitioners, which often they keep secret and disclose them only to a very few of the inner circle of their students.

However tempting it may appear to get to know these secret formulae, a good understanding of the principles of the Taoist Cosmology on which all Feng Shui is based, is of still greater value. Such an understanding, combined with an investigating mind enabling the student to have a fresh and analytical approach, will lead to mastery of this art.

The traditional transmission of knowledge from generation to generation, often in a very exclusive atmosphere may have often prevented critical thought to be applied. Methods correct and useful at earlier times are occasionally, in the changed living conditions of present times, not applicable.

The valid method of avoiding areas having malevolent energy e.g. is difficult to apply in today's modern urban living conditions. At earlier times one simply avoided malevolent energy, which today we cannot afford. Today we have to use the system of the Five Elements to cure an area of its malevolent energy.

Similarly the much talked of support for energies by environmental structures is still given excessively much importance. The influences of environmental structures are a reality, but they are not as important as we often are made to believe. They are the domain of Form School Feng Shui. Flying Star Feng Shui recognizes them, but mainly deals with harmonizing the energies within the building.

Being an ancient traditional system Feng Shui developed many different methods to answer the needs brought about by changes in our living conditions. We should make use of those methods suitable for the present conditions in which we have to live now.

Flying Star Feng Shui correctly understood provides us with a perfect system to diagnose the energies of our environment and to harmonize these energies for improved living.

What is Feng Shui?

Feng Shui is an ancient Chinese method to harness benevolent global directional energy and to counteract malevolent directional energy for the prosperity and well being of people.

Different Feng Shui systems use different methods to determine the energies of a place, burial site, residential or other buildings based on directional exposures, time and environmental factors.

The methods seem often on first view to contradict each other, but comparing them on basis of the fundamentals of the Taoist cosmology one can see their individual value, which make some more and others less promising.

Flying Star Feng Shui

Flying Star School is the most developed system of Feng Shui. It enables us to diagnose and, if necessary, cure the energies present in any individual site or building, taking into account the fluctuations of energy in time on the basis of 9 time periods and the influence of the structure of a site or building which determines its exposure to directional energies.

The time factor given by the period of construction and the exposure of the site or building to directional energies rearrange these energies within the site or building in an individual way. By working out a geomantic chart for a building we get to know its energies. Applying the system of the Five Elements we can harmonize the energies, enhance what is benevolent and reduce the malevolent.

Form School Feng Shui

This is believed to be the oldest school of Feng Shui based on the study of environmental structures and their influence to direct and concentrate beneficial energy in certain locations and to recognize structures creating harmful energy. One could say that rivers, bodies of water and mountains of various shapes are the flying Stars of the Landscape changing the global directional energies into individual energies of the location.

Other schools of Feng Shui, which developed later, such as the Flying Star Method, also pay attention to environmental structures which most of them consider essential to support a building's individual directional energies. Some even hold the view that a building's directional energies, without the support of appropriate environmental structures, are powerless to produce any desirable effect. This, in my view, is not correct, which will be explained in the following chapters.

Eight Mansion Formula

The Eight Mansion Formula is a system based on the dominating energy prevailing on a person's date of birth, to determine in which way the energies of the eight compass directions influence a person's life.

This is worked out independently of any environmental influences such as the prevalent energies in a building and structures in the immediate environment.

What is Directional Energy?

All of us know the magnetic field of the earth as an energy manifest in and depending on a certain direction. The ancient Chinese system of Feng Shui has detailed knowledge of more such directional energies and uses different methods to harness benevolent directional energy and to counteract malevolent directional energy for the prosperity and well being of people.

The directional energies of a site or building are based on directional exposure, time and environmental factors.

Different schools use different methods to determine and influence these energies. The methods often, on first view, seem to contradict each other, but comparing them on the basis of the Taoist cosmology, one can see their individual value

Environmental Structures

Environmental structures are either natural or man-made. They can be mountains, buildings, trees, rivers, lakes, roads, power lines, poles and anything which on account of its shape or activity such as e.g. flowing water or the traffic on a road, can influence the directional energy.

The Influence of Environmental Structures

Environmental structures may enhance or bloc the flow of Directional Energy and can even cause Sha Chi which is energy rushing from a direction and which on account of its pointedness and speed has a harmful effect.

When exposed to a gentle breeze or a draft of air you will feel a difference. Although in both cases it is wind, the gentle breeze will refresh you whereas being exposed to a draft you may fall ill.

Environmental structures may also influence the yin / yang character of directional energy. While a body of water allows extension and therefore represents yang energy, a mountain or tall building narrows space and thereby contracts energy making it predominantly yin in character. This way environmental structures will influence the energy of a building by supporting its yin (Mountain Stars) or yang (Facing Stars) energies.

The very building in which we live has also to be seen as an environmental structure influencing energies. Depending on the building's period of construction and its exposure to the directional energies of the eight compass directions, these energies get altered inside that building.

Yin and Yang

The translation of these two Chinese terms poses a problem. Any of the terms used in other languages conveys only a fraction of the whole meaning of yin and yang.
Yang is: Lower lying ground, a body of water, unobstructed view, light, activity, warmed, growth, movement and noise,
Yin is: Higher lying ground, darkness, decay, coldness, inactivity, and obstructions such as mountains, walls and tall trees.
Translating yang as expansion and yin as contraction in my view is the best we can do, unless we use a whole list of terms for each of these two Chinese concepts.

The Energies in a Palace

In Flying Star Feng Shui the energies in a building are defined by the building's birth date and its directional exposure to the environment from which the dominant maximum yang energy can enter.

The energies distribute themselves, according to a certain pattern into 9 distinct areas of the building generally called palaces. Each palace has basically three different energies. These are the Earth Base or Time Star, the Facing or Water Star and the Mountain or Sitting Star.

The Time Star represents the energy of the period in which the building was completed. The Facing Star represents the directional yang energy to which the building is exposed and the Mountain Star is the directional yin energy.

The terms yin and yang energy in this connection refer only to the polarity of the directional energy to which the building is exposed. The energy of the Facing Star in each of the palaces has dominant yang characteristics and behaves in a yang fashion. The energy of the Mountain Star in each of the palaces has dominant yin characteristics and behaves in a yin way. Some schools have based their whole system on the yin/yang polarity of these two stars and greatly disregard the energy of the Time Star. Other schools pay more attention to the Facing and Time Star since these two stars are seen as possessing the strongest energy, which therefore has also the strongest influence on our lives. They however do not ignore the Mountain Star.

The Annual and Monthly Stars

The Annual and Monthly Stars are visiting energies. The Annual Stars change with the beginning of each Chinese lunar year and the Monthly Stars with each Chinese month. Their influence on the Facing, Earth Base and Mountain Stars is of secondary importance, but should be studied.

We should always pay attention on Annual and Monthly Stars having the numbers 2, 5 and 9 and should apply countermeasures for them. Consider first the influence, which the Annual and Monthly Stars have on the Earth Base Star. Thereafter consider the influence on the Facing Star and then on the Mountain Star

The Annual Stars

2004

Example
Chart of a Period 7 Building facing N2/3 in 2001 with Annual Star 8

1 6	6 8	8 6
6	2	4
7	3	5
9 5	2 3	4 1
5	7	9
6	8	1
5 9	7 7	3 2
1	3	8
2	4	9

The method used to determine the required countermeasures is based on the interaction of the Five Elements (see The System of the Five Elements).

The SE Palace: The Annual Star 7 interacts with Earth Base 6 which creates a combination known to cause armed robbery and injuries. Use water as countermeasure.

The interaction with the other stars in the palace is of no consequence.

The S Palace: The Annual Star interacts with Earth Base 2 which creates a combination causing extreme disharmony and quarrels. It also interacts with the Facing star unfavorably. Use water as countermeasure. Some schools use fire.

SW Place: The annual Star 5 is a very harmful influence in the palace, but the Facing Star 6 drains it of all its energy and therefore nothing needs to be done. As an extra precaution metal can be used.

W Palace: The annual Star 1 reinforces the energy of the Facing Star 1, counters the energy of the malevolent Earth Base 9 and nourishes the Mountain Star 4. The influence of the Annual Star is positive in this palace.

NW Palace: The Annual Star 9 nourishes both the Facing and the Earth Base and depletes the energy of the Mountain Star 3. The nourishing effect it has on the Facing Star 2 is undesirable. Use water or metal as countermeasure.

N Palace: The Annual Star 4 interacting with the Earth Base 3 creates perfect harmony of yin and yang. The influence of the Annual Star in this palace does not require any countermeasure.

NE Palace: The Annual Star 2 destroys the energy of the Earth Base 1 and depletes the energy of the Facing Star 9. In combination with the Mountain Star 5 it is a very dangerous force. Use metal as countermeasure.

E Palace: The Annual Star 6 drains the energy of the Earth base and the Facing Star, which is very desirable. Nothing needs to be done.

Table of Calendar Years – Annual Stars – First Monthly Stars

2000	9	5		2010	8	2		2020	7	8
2001	8	2		2011	7	8		2021	6	5
2002	7	8		2012	6	5		2022	5	2
2003	6	5		2013	5	2		2023	4	8
2004	5	2		2014	4	8		2024	3	5
2005	4	8		2015	3	5		2025	2	2
2006	3	5		2016	2	2		2026	1	8
2007	2	2		2017	1	8		2027	9	5
2008	1	8		2018	9	5		2028	8	2
2009	9	5		2019	8	2		2029	7	8

Sequence of Lunar Months and their Ruling Stars

1st Lunar Month Star	8
2nd Lunar Month Star	7
3rd Lunar Month Star	6
4th Lunar Month Star	5
5th Lunar Month Star	4
6th Lunar Month Star	3
7th Lunar Month Star	2
8th Lunar Month Star	1
9th Lunar Month Star	9
10th Lunar Month Star	8
11th Lunar Month Star	7
12th Lunar Month Star	6

In the year 2002 the rule of the Annual Star 7 and of the First Monthly Star 8 started on February 12th.
Please remember, the Annual Star and the First Monthly Star start on Chinese New Year of the respective Calendar Year

The Monthly Stars

To assess the interaction of the Monthly Stars in a palace you proceed in the same way as was done with the Annual Stars. You first examine the interaction of the Monthly Star with the Earth Base Star and the Facing Star. Thereafter consider the interaction it has with the Annual Star and the Mountain Star.

As you will see the matter becomes more complicated having now five energies to consider in their interaction. Do concentrate on how the Monthly Stars numbers 2, 5 and 9 interact with the Earth Base and the Facing Star.

Different Schools apply different Systems

In the Application of the Monthly Stars two different Systems are used.

1.) Some schools fly **all Monthly Stars of a year** in an ascending (yang) way in the chart.

2.) Other schools fly the Stars from the first Lunar Month onward in an ascending (yang) way, **but from the Lunar Month in which summer solstice falls onward** up to the end of the Lunar Year in a descending (yin) way.

<table>
<tr><td colspan="3">Example
for flying the Monthly
Stars ascending</td><td></td><td colspan="3">Example
for flying the Monthly Stars
descending</td></tr>
</table>

7	3	5		5	9	7
6	8	1		6	4	2
2	4	9		1	8	3

Example

In the year 2002 Chinese New Year falls on the 12th of February. From this date onward up to the end of this Lunar Year, the Annual Star 7 will rule.

The first Lunar Month starting on the same date, has the number 8. In the first four months of the Chinese Lunar Year the Monthly Stars fly ascending.

Summer solstice is on the 21st of June and falls in the 5th Chinese Lunar Month, which has the number 4. In the 5th Lunar Month the Monthly Star number 4 is therefore flying descending and so do all stars of the Lunar Months for the rest of the year.

.

Yin and Yang in the Cycle of a Year

While the first method does not observe the waxing and waning of yin and yang in the cycle of a year, the second method takes this into account. Schools using the second method adjust their ways to the changes the cosmic energy undergoes in the cycle of a year which is necessary to keep tuned to realities.

The Geomantic Chart

Once the period of a building and its Facing Direction are known, we can work out a Geomantic Chart to see how the directional energies have been individually rearranged in the building by its exposure to the energies of the eight compass directions and the period of the building's construction.

The Time Factor

The energies, which are known to be present in the eight compass directions, rearrange themselves in accordance with a certain pattern depending on the buildings period of construction. They are known as the Earth Base or Time Stars.

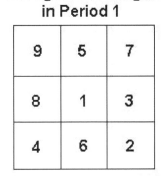

Energies of the 8 Compass Directions

4	9	2
3	5	7
8	1	6

Energies rearranged in Period 1

9	5	7
8	1	3
4	6	2

The Directional Exposure

The directional exposure, the so-called Facing Direction, is the direction from which energy enters a building and spreads throughout following the same pattern as the Earth Base Stars do.

The energy present in the Facing Palace is put on the right side of the Earth Base Star in the Center Palace and is called the Facing Star. Opposite to the Facing Direction is the Sitting Direction. The energy present in the Sitting Palace is put on the left side of the Earth Base Star and is called Mountain or Sitting Star.

The energy of the Facing and the Mountain Stars can spread in a yin (descending) or a yang (ascending) fashion depending on which of the three subsections of any of the eight compass directions the building is facing. In the example below the building is facing subsection 1 of the W. the Facing Stars (blue) spread in a yang fashion and the Mountain Stars (red) spread in a yin fashion.

Pattern in which energy spreads

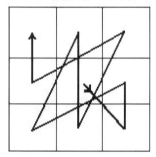

Energies rearranged in Period 1 with Facing Direction W 1

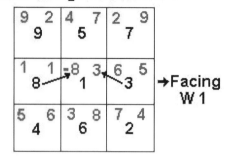

In order to know, if the Facing and/or Mountain Star of a given period and Facing Direction move in a yin or yang fashion, please refer to the following 9 diagrams. The numbers in the center indicate the periods. Each of the eight compass directions has the Earth Base Stars representing the energy as they are rearranged by the period. The three subsections of each compass direction have a + (yang) or a – (yin) sign indicating in which fashion the energy spreads.

With the help of these diagrams one can work out Geomantic Charts for buildings of all 9 periods and all 24 Facing Directions.

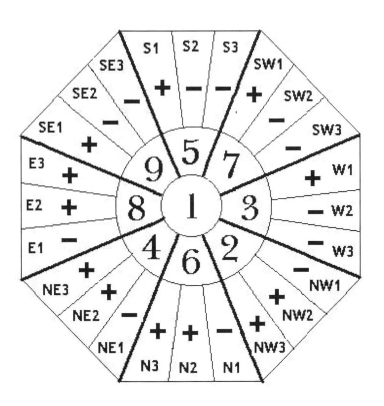

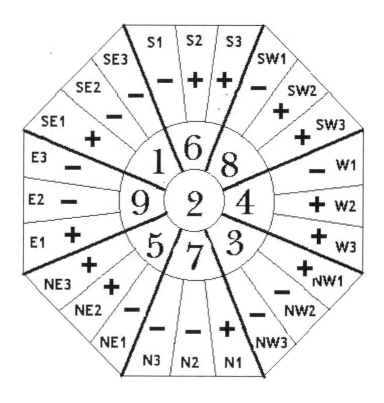

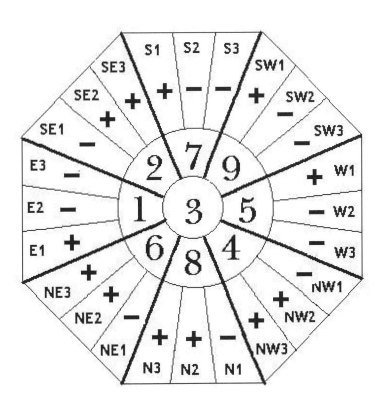

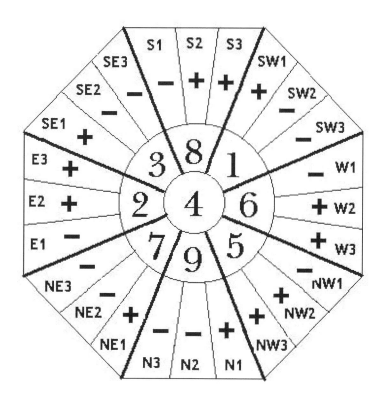

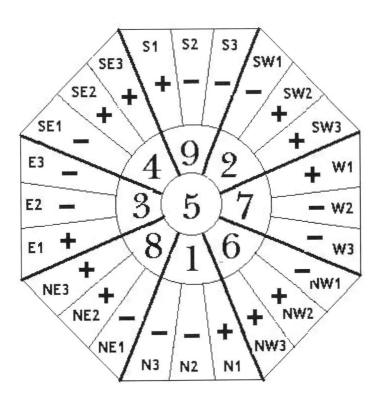

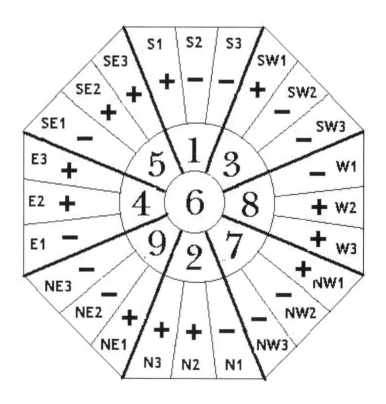

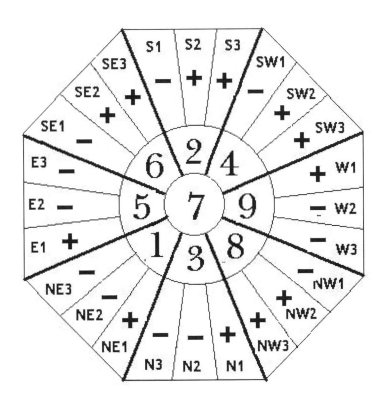

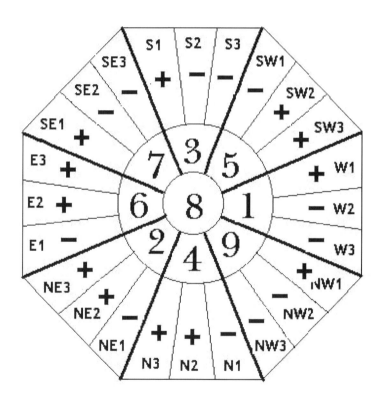

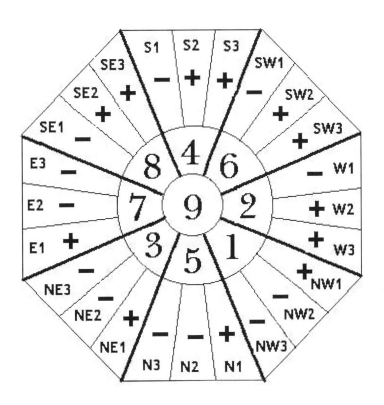

The 9 Periods

The time factor in Feng Shui is made up of 9 periods of 20 years each, which make a whole cycle of 180 years.

Each period starts on the first day of a Chinese lunar year. Period 8 e.g. starts on Chinese New Year in 2004 and lasts to the day before Chinese New Year in 2024.

Period 1 1864 to 1884
Period 2 1884 to 1904
Period 3 1904 to 1924
Period 4 1924 to 1944
Period 5 1944 to 1964
Period 6 1964 to 1984
Period 7 1984 to 2004
Period 8 2004 to 2024
Period 9 2024 to 2044
Period 1 2044 to 2064
Period 2 2064 to 2104

The energy symbolized by the numbers 1 to 9 is believed to be strongest during the reign of the period, which has the same number (see under Timeliness of Energy).

The Facing Direction

To determine the Facing Direction is at times the easiest most straightforward thing, but it can also be the most difficult task to perform which needs a lot of experience and a thorough knowledge of the fundamentals.

The Facing Direction is the direction from which maximum yang energy enters through the face of the building at an angle of 90°. The front of a building facing the greatest amount of yang energy is the face of the building, provided energy can enter the face of the building through entrances, large windows and/or doors.

Yang stands for expansion, activity warmed, growth and light. The immediate environment of the building has to be examined for it to find the direction in which yang is predominant.

Apart from this the general shape and structure of the building have to be considered to identify the face of a building since energy will penetrate through a large front better and easier than through a small one. We have to identify the front of the building, which is largest, has the largest and most used entrance and/or the most windows. If this front is also exposed to the maximum yang energy of the environment, it will be the face of the building. Most buildings are like that.

Should the general shape and exposure of the building and the direction of maximum yang energy in the environment not be one and the same, we will have to decide on the direction, which looks to be more exposed and open to outside energy.

Last but not least the ease with which energy can spread throughout the building is important.

The Facing Direction of a building or a part of it, such as an apartment or a shop, therefore depends on these three factors:

1. **The direction in which the external environment is predominantly yang in nature.**
2. **The exposure of the building or part of it to the external environment**
3. **The internal structure of a building or part of it, which enables the energies to spread to all sectors of it.**

The Facing Direction of a building may very often be the direction of the entrance, since the use of the entrance activates the intake of energy, but need not necessarily be so. It is the direction from which the maximum yang energy of the environment can enter the building easily and spread throughout it.

To determine the Facing Direction of a single unit in a building, such as an apartment or a shop depends on the way energy enters the unit. We first of all have to find out if energy enters by way of the building's Facing Direction or if it enters from a direction independent of the buildings Facing Direction. This can be a very challenging task.

If a single unit such as an apartment can take in energy from more than one direction as e.g. the buildings Facing Direction, as well as through large windows, we very carefully have to find out which energy is the dominating one.

The External Environment

Water as such and because it is found in lower lying ground, is understood to be a strong yang factor in the external environment. Lower lying ground also is yang, because it allows expansion as is evident in the far-reaching view it owns. A mountain, a manmade structure or higher lying ground limits and hinders expansion and the direction of its location is therefore understood to be predominantly yin in nature.

The Exposure of the Building or Part of it

This is the front of the building or of a single unit of it, which allows by way of main doors, entrances, openings or windows, the directional energies to enter.

The Internal Structure of a Building or Part of it

This is the factor which enables energy which entered the building or single unit of it to spread throughout all sectors in an easy way. This is especially to be considered when more than one direction qualifies as Facing Direction on account of exposure to maximum yang energy of the immediate environment. The direction from which energy can spread easiest to all parts of the building will be the Facing Direction.

Facing Directions have Dominant Energy

A Facing Direction is the direction of 90° from the front of a building, which is exposed to the strongest yang energy of the immediate environment and able to allow entry of that energy by way of entrances openings and windows.

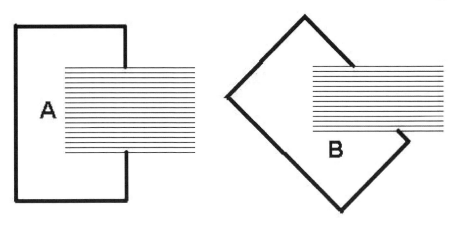

Buildings A and B have Openings of Equal Size through which Energy can enter.

Energy, which enters a building (A) from the Facing Direction is stronger than any other energy and is therefore the dominating energy of a building.

Energy, which enters a building (B) at its Facing Front in an angle other than 90°, does not have the same strength.

The Complexity of finding the Facing Directions of modern Office and Apartment Buildings

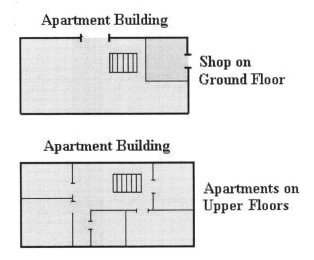

The Facing Direction of the shop on the ground floor is independent from the Facing Direction of the building since the energy, which enters the building, cannot spread to the shop.

The Facing Direction of the apartments on the upper floors that are connected to each other and the ground floor by a staircase, receive the energy, which has entered the building through the buildings Facing Direction. They all may share the Facing Direction of the building.

Two Storied Apartment Building

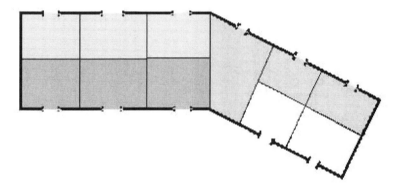

The building has no common entrance. Each unit has it's own entrance and there are no doors connecting any of the units. Each unit has therefore it's own Facing Direction. Units marked in the same color share the same Facing Direction.

Apartment Building with Common Entrance

First 3 floors are open on all sides and are used for parking cars. All other floors have residential units and are connected by an open staircase. A lift serves all floors.

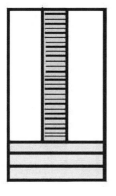 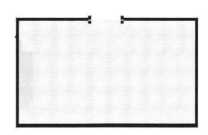

Side view of the Building   Ground floor of the Building

The Facing Direction of the first 3 floors is the direction of the common entrance of the apartment building. It is the direction from which energy enters by the traffic of residents and cars entering the building.

The Upper Floors

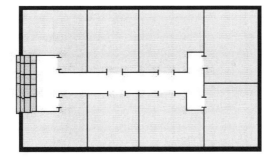

The Facing Direction for the rest of the floors is determined by the direction of the open staircase serving these floors. Energy enters from the direction of the staircase and spreads to all units of each respective floor. The direction of the open staircase may very well be the Facing Direction of all residential units of each of these floors, but we also have to consider the intake of energy through the windows of each unit. The direction from which the dominating energy enters will be the Facing Direction.

25

Office Building Having Glass Facades on all four Sides

Common Entrance on the Ground Floor. Six Elevators and one Stair Case serve all upper Floors

Ground Floor

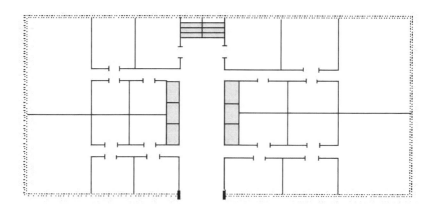

All Upper Floors

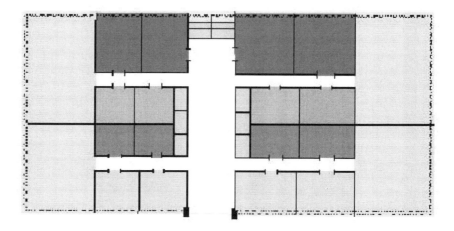

The Facing Direction of the ground floor is the direction of the common entrance. The traffic of many people through the common entrance and an open wide parking

ground in front of it, satisfies the requirement of a predominantly yang external environment and an excellent exposure to it. The internal structure of the ground floor permits the energy to spread to all units. The different ground floor units therefore share the Facing Direction of the building.

The Facing Directions of units on all upper floors are determined by each unit's exposure to the external environment. The lifts are not suited to spread the energy from the ground floor to the upper floors. The staircase connecting all floors allows energy, which enters through the common entrance, to spread to the upper floors but the glass fronts on all four sides of the building also permit energy to enter and this energy is likely to be stronger and therefore dominant.

All four directions of the building are predominantly yang since the upper floors face lower lying ground all around. We therefore can assume that of both energies, the energy that enters through the common entrance and spreads to the upper floors and the energy, which enters through the glass front of the building, the later one is likely to be stronger and dominant. We will therefore have Facing Directions as follows:

The units marked in gray have their window frontage in the same direction as the entrance on the ground floor and therefore share the ground floor's Facing Direction.

The units marked in purple face the opposite direction, which is therefore also their Facing Direction.

The units marked in yellow have two directions to choose from. The larger window frontage of the two of each unit has the advantage to allow more energy to enter, but the decision has to be made on the nature of the external environment. The window front facing the direction which is more yang in nature will qualify as Facing Direction.

The units marked in red have no windows and therefore no access to competing energy. Their energy enters through their doors. The direction of their doors and the direction of the common entrance on the ground floor are the same and so are their Facing Directions.

The units marked in green have no windows and therefore no access to competing energy. We may therefore assume that their energy, which enters through their doors, is the dominant energy and the direction of their doors may be their Facing Direction.

Applying the Geomantic Chart on the Floor Plan

The geomantic chart should be applied to cover the whole of the floor plan. Buildings, which are L or U shaped or irregular in any other way, will have palaces of the geomantic chart missing in the floor plan. When more than half of a palace is not covered by the floor plan the energies of that palace are considered to be missing in the building.

The correct application of the geomantic chart on the floor plan below shows two palaces marked in green, which are not covered by the floor plan. The energies of these palaces are therefore missing in the building.

Any other application of the geomantic chart, which doesn't cover the whole of the floor plan, is wrong. The geomantic chart does not cover areas of the floor plan, which are marked in yellow.

Correct Application

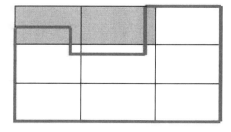

Wrong Application

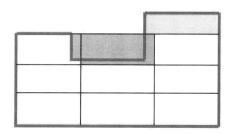

Correct Application

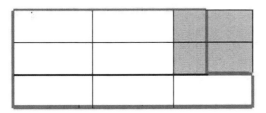

Wrong Application

The Position of the Facing Palace in the Geomantic Chart

Always remember, the Facing Direction is a direction and not a location. The Facing Palace corresponds to the Facing Direction.

Position of Facing Palace marked in blue for Facing Direction S 2 (180°) taken at the Location of the Main Entrance

SE	S		SW
E	C		W
NE	N		NW

Position of Facing Palace marked in blue for Facing Direction S 2 (180°) taken at the Location of the Main Entrance

SE	S	SW
E	C	W
NE	N	NW

Position of Facing Palace marked in blue for Facing Direction SE 1 (120°) taken at the Location of the Main Entrance

E	SE	S
NE	C	SW
N	NW	W

This Position of the Facing Palace for Facing Direction SE 1 (120°) taken at the Location of the Main Entrance is wrong.

This is a wrong Positioning of the Facing Palace

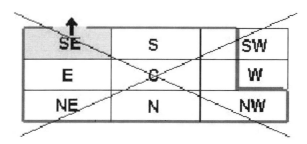

Position of Facing Palace marked in blue for Facing Direction NW 3 (300°) taken at the Location of the Main Entrance.
Since less than one half of the S and the E Palaces are covered by the Floor plan, the energies of these palaces are not in the   Building

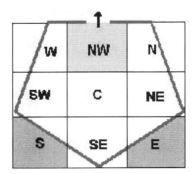

Position of Facing Palace marked in blue for Facing Direction E 2 (90°) taken at the Location of the two Entrances.
The Facing Palace is not covered by the Floor Plan. Of the NW and SW Palaces less than one half is covered by the Floor Plan. The Energies of the NW, SW and Facing Palace are missing in the Building.

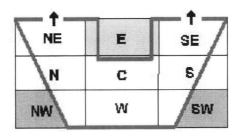

Problems with the Period

In order to draw a geomantic chart to get the distribution of energies in a building we need the following information:

- The Facing Direction of the building
- The period of the building

Regarding the period three systems are in use:

- Time of construction of the building
- Time of moving into the building
- Current period

Time of Construction of the Building

The majority of Feng Shui consultants uses the period in which the building was constructed. It is based on the understanding that the energy of the prevailing period at the time of construction is dominant.

The global directional energies at the time of construction get rearranged by the time factor into the prevailing period's distribution of these energies. This process is comparable to the casting of a horoscope based on the position of the planets at the time of birth.

Changes in the construction or extensive renovations in a later period may again change the distribution of the global energies according to that period. It requires a lot of experience to evaluate such a situation.

Time of moving into the building

This method is based on the assumption that the energies of heaven, earth and man have to come together to complete the individual energy setup of a building. This is seen to be realized when residents are moving in. It is believed that any change in residents or a vacancy of the building for at least 100 days can change the buildings period.

Current period

This method is based on the idea that the energy distribution of each period overrides any other distribution of the global energies and that all buildings change their energy distribution with the onset of a new period.

Problems with the Facing Direction

As we have seen, it can be very difficult to determine the Facing Direction of a building.

When two or more directions qualify as the Facing Direction of a building or single unit of it and we cannot decide for one of them, it is advisable to use multiple charts.

Multiple charts should also be used when the period of a building is not certain. This can often happen when the construction of the building took place at the time of period change or when renovations were done during different periods.

There is still another Problem regarding the Facing Direction. When the Facing Direction is within 3° of the dividing line between two of the 24 compass directions, the energies may intermingle. In such cases the system of Replacement Stars is applied (see under Replacement Stars).

Multiple Charts

Sometimes we are advised to use more than one chart to diagnose the energies of a building. This may look strange, since by all reasoning only one chart can be the correct one. However there are situations when multiple charts are required. They are used whenever, one or both,

1. **The Facing Direction, or**
2. **The Period of a Building**

are not certain (see under Problems with the Facing Directions and Problems with Period).

Under circumstances when one cannot be certain of either the Period or the Facing Direction, multiple charts may be required to assess the energies of a building. In such cases multiple charts will act as safety devices by considering the energies indicated by the "other" chart as well. This may also be necessary most frequently, when trying to find the Facing Direction of a single unit in an apartment building. According to the principle of the unity of things in the cosmos, the microcosm reflects the macrocosm. A unit in a building is therefore the microcosm of the whole building, which represents the macrocosm. However, the unit on account of the floor plan and its own individual special exposure to the immediate environment may suggest a Facing Direction independent of the Facing Direction of the whole Building. In such a case the different charts reflecting both Facing Directions should be used.

Very often after analysing both charts one will realize that one of them suits the situations of the occupants of the unit, while the other one does not. A decision on the Facing Direction can then easily be made. The chart suiting the situation will have the correct Facing Direction.

If however confusion persists, the method below will assure that harm is avoided.

The method applied to analyse the stars in the different palaces of the chart in their interaction will be explained and dealt with in detail in the chapter on "the interaction of the five elements".

Two Competing Facing Directions

Let us look at the example of a house build in period 7. The house has two directions, S1 and E1, which qualify as Facing Directions.

The chart S1 has beneficial Stars in the N, NE, NW and S palace and malevolent stars and star combinations in the E, SE, SW, W, and C palace.

The chart E1 has beneficial stars in the, NW, SE and to a lesser degree in the NE palace and malevolent stars and star combinations in the E, SW, W, S, N, and C palace.

Step 1 : Compare palaces with benevolent stars in both charts. These are the NE and NW palaces in this example. The numbers of the stars below are in the order of Mountain/Earth Base/Facing Star.

In the NE Palace the Chart S1 has the stars 6/1/8 and the chart E1 has the stars 3/1/8.

In the NW Palace Chart S1 has the stars 4/8/1 and chart E1 has the stars 1/8/6.

According to the nature of the stars present, you can safely recommend rooms in these areas to be used as bedrooms, family rooms and home offices. Occupants, except small children, should spend most of their time in these areas.

Step 2 : Compare the rest of the palaces with beneficial stars of each chart with the corresponding palaces of the other chart.

1.) The N palace of Chart S1 has the stars 8/3/6, which is an excellent combination.

The N palace of chart E1 has the stars 5/3/1. Here, the excellent Facing Star 1 makes this a good palace when metal is used as a countermeasure to deal with the Mountain Star 5. A metal countermeasure will not harm the good stars of the N Palace of the S1 Chart. The N Palace can therefore also be recommended as a bedroom, family room or home office, where occupants spend a lot of time.

2.) S Palace of Chart S1 has the stars 7/2/7 which is basically very good for a period 7 house and because the combination 7/2 represents the fire element, which has its place in the S.

The S palace of chart E1 has the stars 4/2/9. The combination Earth Base 2 and Facing Star 9 is very malevolent. The countermeasure here should be water.

Water as countermeasure will on the other hand reduce the auspicious double 7 in the palace and douse the fire element combination 2/7 of chart S1. The area is therefore not recommended for important rooms. A storeroom or guest room could be there.

The SE palace in chart E1 has the stars 8/6/4, which is an excellent combination.

The SE palace of chart S1 has the stars 2/6/3, which on account of the 3/2 is very bad and would require fire as countermeasure. This countermeasure would harm Facing Star 4 and Earth Base Star 6 of chart E1, but not Mountain Star 8. Comparing the situation in both charts, the area, after applying countermeasures is all right, but not recommended for important rooms.

Step 3 : Compare the rest of the palaces. You will find that all palaces except the C Palace in chart S1 have either a Star 2 or 5 or even combinations of 2 or 5 with 9 which are all malevolent. The C Palace in chart S1 has the combination of 2/3, which is a serious flaw. The same palace in chart E1 with the combination 9/7/5 is even worse

For Palace SW in Chart S1 having the stars 9/4/5 the countermeasure is water and in Chart E1 having the stars 6/4/2 it is metal.

For Palace E in Chart E1 having the stars 7/5/3 on account of the strength of Earth Base Star 5, it is advisable to use metal.

For Palace E in Chart S1 having the stars 1/5/4 metal should be used.

For Palace W in Chart S1 having the stars 5/9/9 water is needed.

For Palace W in Chart E1 having the stars 2/9/7 water should be applied.

For Palace C in Chart S1 having the stars 3/7/2 water is needed.

For Palace C in Chart E1 having the stars 9/7/5 water is needed.

All areas need countermeasures and none of them can be recommended for important rooms. The areas should be reserved for rooms, which are used rarely and only for short times

When using multiple charts for competing Periods the same method is to be applied.

Having drawn up the geomantic charts, proceed with step1, 2, and 3 as per example above.

Replacement Stars

Replacement Stars are used to replace the Facing and Mountain Stars of a chart when the Facing Direction is close to the borderline of another one of the 24 compass directions.

When the Facing Direction of a building is within 3° of the borderline of another direction (mountains), such as N1 bordering N2 or N3 bordering NE1, the energies of both directions intermingle. To arrive at a correct chart of the energies in such a case, the Replacement Star Formula is used. This system gives a new set of stars in the nine palaces called Replacement Stars to depict the true effect of the mixed energies.

The Earth Base energy, depending only on the time factor of the period, remains the same, but the Facing and Mountain Stars have to be changed.

The Formula

Compass Directions (Mountains)	Replacement Stars
Zi, Gui, Jia, Shen	Tan
N2, N3, E1, SW3	1
Mao, Yi, Wei, Kun, Ren	Ju
E2, E3, SW1, SW2, N1	2
Chen, Xu, Qian, Hai, Xun, Si	Wu
SE1, SE2, SE3, NW1, NW2, NW3	6
You, Xin, Chou, Gen, Bing	Po
W2, W3, NE1, NE2, S1	7
Wu, Ding, Yin, Geng	Bi
S2, S3, NE3, W1	9

Later Heaven and Replacement Stars

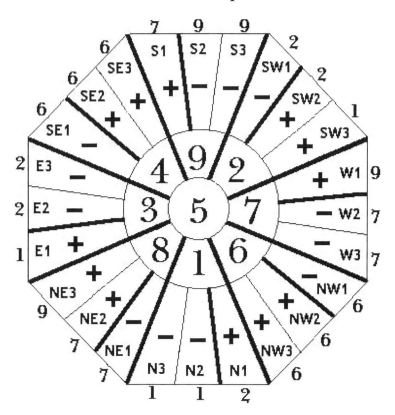

The Method
Example

A period 6 building facing 249 °, which means it, is facing W1 bordering SW3.

Period 6 Facing W1

	-4 -8 6	

Replacement Star

	-6 -7 6	

Flying the Stars gives below Charts

Period 6 Facing W1

5 9 5	9 4 1	7 2 3
6 1 4	-4 -8 6	2 6 8
1 5 9	8 3 2	3 7 7

Replacement Star

7 8 5	2 3 1	9 1 3
8 9 4	-6 -7 6	4 5 8
3 4 9	1 2 2	5 6 7

To find the Replacement Stars follow these steps:

Step1: Look at chart of "Later Heaven and Replacement Stars" and locate star number 8 from the inner circle in the diagram, which is in the NE 1 and NE 2/3 positions.

Step 2: Since the building is facing the first subsection of W and the Facing Star number 8 flies (yin) descending, you select the Replacement Star from the first sub section of the NE which is number 7 and will also fly (yin) descending.

Follow the same procedure to find the replacement Star for the Mountain Star number 4.

Step 1: Locate star number 4 in the chart of the "Later Heaven and the Replacement Stars", which is in the SE1 and SE 2/3 positions.

Step 2: Since the building is the Sitting Direction of E1 and the mountain Star is flying (yin), you select the Replacement Star from the first sub section of the SE which is number 6 and will also fly (yin) descending.

While all compass directions have replacement Stars some are of the same number and others have a different number. The number 5 positioned in the center has no direction and has therefore no Replacement Star.

Directions not requiring Replacement Stars

Not all Facing Directions, which are within 3° of another direction (mountain), require Replacement Stars.

Facing Directions which are within 3° of another direction sharing the same number (belonging to the same trigram) and flying in the same way descending (yin) or ascending (yang) do not require Replacement Stars since both directions have the same energies.

In the Diagram above, these directions meet at **thin dividing lines.**

These are the following Directions

Facing Direction N2 within 3° of Direction N3
Facing Direction N3 within 3° of Direction N2
Facing Direction S2 within 3° of Direction S3
Facing Direction S3 within 3° of Direction S2
Facing Direction W2 within 3° of Direction W3
Facing Direction W3 within 3° of Direction W2
Facing Direction E2 within 3° of Direction E3
Facing Direction E3 within 3° of Direction E2
Facing Direction NE2 within 3° of Direction NE3
Facing Direction NE3 within 3° of Direction NE2
Facing Direction SE2 within 3° of Direction SE3
Facing Direction SE3 within 3° of Direction SE2

Facing Direction SW2 within 3° of Direction SW3
Facing Direction SW3 within 3° of Direction SW2
Facing Direction NW2 within 3° of Direction NW3
Facing Direction NW3 within 3° of Direction NW2

All other directions within 3° of another direction, meeting at **thick dividing lines** in the diagram, require Replacement Stars.

When to use Replacement Stars

When the Facing Direction is only 3° or less away from the borderline to the next direction an influence by the neighboring energies is possible.
The use of Replacement Stars is much disputed among different masters. In general we can say that Replacement Stars are to be used, when the Facing Direction is only 3° or less away from the borderline to the next direction (mountain), since some influence by the neighboring energies seems possible.

Some masters however claim that the energies of a direction (mountain) are very stable and will not be influenced by the energies of the neighbouring direction and therefore will not use Replacement Stars when the Facing Direction is 3° or less away from the borderline.

They will use Replacement Stars only when the Facing Direction is directly on the dividing line between two directions.

When Facing Directions are directly on the dividing line between two directions, an intermingling of energies takes place.

Facing Directions exactly on dividing lines between two directions within a trigram such as N1 and N2 will have an intermingling of energies. The different ascending or descending way, in which the Facing and Mountain Stars are flying in the charts, causes the difference of the energies of both directions.

Facing Directions exactly on dividing lines between two trigrams such as NW3 and N1 will also have an intermingling of energies. In such cases the difference of the energies is caused by the different trigram numbers and some times by the different way in which the Facing and Mountain Stars are flying in the chart. The difference of the intermingling energies is therefore much greater.

Masters recommend in such cases to make separate Replacement Star charts for both directions and on the situation experienced by the occupants of the building, decide for one of them. Should it prove difficult to decide for a chart, the method of the multiple charts (see multiple charts for details) could be used.

Many masters seem to agree that Facing Directions directly on the borderline between two directions will cause energies to fight for supremacy, bond in evil combinations or cause undecided situations, which will have negative effects on the occupants and advise them to move out.

However this will depend on the nature of the energies present and may not always be bad. Experience has shown that even in such cases with the correct application of countermeasures the occupants lived successful lives.

Fan Fu Yin Charts

The formation of this chart is given when a Facing or a Mountain Star number 5 is in the Center Palace. The Fan Fu Yin Chart is held to be very unfortunate. Different reasons for the unfortunate character of this chart are given. Some of them are rather bizarre and a matter of belief. There is however one convincing explanation which can be understood and accepted.

Later Heaven

4	9	2
3	5	7
8	1	6

According to the Cosmic Order of the Later Heaven arrangement of energies the 5 is in the center and has no trigram. The energy of a star number 5 is undefined in its yin/yang components and on account of this is not stable but very volatile and its character is therefore understood to be malevolent.

When a number 5 Facing or Mountain Star is in the Center Palace their energy is in its due place of the Later Heaven arrangement and is therefore dominant and intervening with the distribution of the Period Star energy.

Flying Star Feng Shui deals with the dominant energies in a chart. These are as a rule the energies of the Facing, Mountain, Earth Base, Annual and Monthly Stars. The underlying reality of the Later Heaven arrangement of energies is however always present and should not be ignored. This is e.g. evident in the location of the Ho Tu number combinations as well as in some star combinations in certain palaces.

E.g. the Ho Tu number combination of 1/6, which represents the water element when found in the E or SE Palaces will enhance the wood element of number 3 and 4 and thereby promotes successful studies and research.

The star combination 8/2 when found in the NW Palace is an indication for tremendous wealth. Facing Star 8 and Earth Base 2 combined represent a very powerful earth element, which will enhance the metal element of number 6 in the Later Heaven arrangement. Having a Facing or Mountain Star 5 in the Center Palace enhances the energies as distributed in the Later Heaven arrangement, which interfere with the distribution of the dominant Period Energies and thereby causes obstructions.

Fan Fu Yin Charts are divided into:

1. Fan Yin Charts which have a Facing or Mountain Star number 5 Flying (yin) descending and
2. Fu Yin Charts in which the number 5 Facing or Mountain Star flies (yang) ascending.

Fan Fu Yin in a Three Combination Chart or in a Combination of Ten Chart will not have any negative effect and can be ignored.

Remedies for Fan Fu Yin Charts

1.) Change of Facing Direction

If possible one should change the Facing Direction to get rid of a Facing or Mountain Star number 5 in the Center Palace.
Moving the main door or a large window can do this if either of them is accountable for the Facing Direction.
If environmental factors such as lower lying open ground, a road or a body of water are vital factors for the Facing Direction, a wall, bushes or trees can be used to block off these features.

2.) Inviting the Strongest Energy to the Center Palace

If changing the Facing Direction is not feasible the strongest energy available must be directed to the Center Palace.
The strongest energy will be in the Facing Star having the number of the current ongoing period. This star has to be activated with a water feature. The flow of water should be in the direction of the Center Palace. Make sure that a clear unobstructed path between this star and the Center Palace makes the flow of energy possible.

Jailed Period Star

The Facing Star and Mountain Star in the Center Palace are said to be jailed in that location and therefore unable to direct the energy of their periods into the building. This condition occurs, when the Facing or Mountain Star in the Center Palace has the number of the prevailing respective period.

The Facing Star and also the Mountain star are understood to direct the period energy into a building but cannot do so when jailed in the Center Palace.

Example of a Period 7 Building facing W 1

4 8 6	9 4 2	2 6 4
3 7 5	5 9 7	7 2 9
8 3 1	1 5 3	6 1 8

A building of the period 7 facing W 1 will have a jailed Facing Star in period 9. In less than 40 years after construction was completed the building will become unfortunate because the energy of period 9 cannot enter the building. This is a very regrettable situation, which will last for the whole 20 years duration of period 9.

However, when period 9 is over and period 1 has started the unlucky situation is over and the period energy of period 1 can enter the building. The same applies to the Mountain Star when jailed in the Center Palace.

Jailed Stars in a Three Combination Chart have no negative effect and do not prevent their respective energies to enter the building.

The Remedy

Changing the Facing Direction, if possible, is the easiest way to remedy a Jailed Star situation. Failing this there is another remedy, which consists of inviting the energy of the prevailing period in which a star is jailed by activating the Facing Star number 5 with a water feature having the flow of water in the direction to the center of the building. This method works only under the condition that a clear unobstructed path between star number 5 and the Center Palace makes the flow of energy to the center possible.

You may think this could create a Fan Fu Yin situation, but it will not. The energy of a number 5 Facing or Mountain Star not having a trigram and therefore being undefined regarding its yin and yang composition is unstable and volatile and adopts the yin/yang composition of the direction of the Later Heaven in which it is placed. A Facing Star number 5 in the E Palace e.g. will therefore have the energy composition of a star number 3.

The Timeliness of Energy

With the change of periods the level of the energy represented by different stars undergoes change. This fact is understood and dealt with in two different ways:

- The Timeliness of Facing and Mountain Stars
- The Waxing and Waning of Earth Base Energy

The Timeliness of Facing and Mountain Stars

Schools, which in the analysis of the energies of a building are mainly concerned with the Facing and Mountain Stars, apply a time factor to these two stars. Depending on the respective current period the stars are interpreted to be positive or negative.

The timeliness of a star is seen as most important. E.g. a star number 7 in the period of 7 is considered activated and benevolent. In period 8 star 7 is retreating and not benevolent any more. This concept of timeliness of the energy of the stars proclaims that the character of the stars as determined by their numbers, changes in different periods.

Level of Energy of the Earth Base, Facing and Mountain Stars according to their timeliness

Energy	The 9 Periods								
of stars	1	2	3	4	5	6	7	8	9
Prosperous	1	2	3	4	5	6	7	8	9
Growing	2 3	3 4	4 5	5 6	6 7	7 8	8 9	9 1	1 2
Retreating	9	1	2	3	4	5	6	7	8
Dead	6 7	9 6	1 6	2 8	2 3	4 9	5 4 3	2 6	6 7
Killing	5	5 7	7 9	7 9	2 9	2 3	2 3	3 4 5	3 4 5

The Waxing and Waning of Earth Base Energy

Schools, which consider all three stars when analyzing the energies of a palace, apply the timeliness to the Earth Base Stars only, which in different periods will be waxing or waning. The Facing and Mountain Stars according to them, do not change their character throughout the 9 cycles, but remain stable in their benevolent or malevolent influence. A Facing or Mountain Star number 7 in the present period of 7, as in all other periods, is therefore considered neutral in the interaction of the stars, but very malevolent in certain combinations. The change in the strength of the Earth Base Star, according to the prevailing period, will only have a modifying effect in the interaction of the stars. An Earth Base Star number 7 in period 7 has a high level of energy but in period 8 the energy is failing.

Level of Energy of the Earth Base Stars in different Periods

Period in which building was constructed

The 9 Periods

	1	2	3	4	5	6	7	8	9
1	high	failing	rising	good	good	good	good	good	good
2	rising	high	failing	dead	dead	dead	neutral	rising	dead
3	neutral	rising	high	failing	destructive.	dead	failing	rising	dead
4	good	good	rising	high	failing	rising	neutral	good	good
5	dead	dead	dead	rising	high	failing	dead	dead	dead
6	good	good	good	good	rising	high	failing	good	good
7	dead	neutral	rising	dead	dead	rising	high	failing	dead
8	good	good	good	good	good	good	rising	high	failing
9	failing	dead	dead	neutral	dead	dead	neutral	rising	high

The Castle Gate Formula

The formula is applicable only for buildings constructed during the respective current period and is based on the timeliness of the energy of the Facing Star.

The formula is used to give buildings constructed during a current period the very best Facing Direction achievable and thereby ensuring the greatest prosperity possible. Making the building part of a larger area, which has a Castle Gate as Facing Direction, changes the Facing Directions of buildings already constructed. According to the formula a Facing Star number 8 in the period 8 is considered very auspicious. When the timely Facing Star is flying descending (yin) and is activated by the presence of water in the Facing Direction it is most auspicious (see chapter on Four Combinations of ascending and descending Facing and Mountain Stars).
The auspicious wealth enhancing property of the formula is applicable only in its own period and only when the building is surrounded by mountains or by higher structures all around leaving open one gap where water can be seen.
The Castle Gate Formula explains from which directions the energy, which is prosperous during a respective period, enters the area and can be enhanced with water.

The Castle Gates are the very best Facing Directions of a period and are grouped in:

1. **The Primary Castle Gates** which are located in directions, which relate to the Facing Direction as Ho Tu number combinations.

2. **The Secondary Castle Gates** do not have that feature. They are therefore of lesser importance and grouped as secondary.

The Castle Gates are related to Facing Directions of buildings in angles of 45°. The formula is generally considered to be one of the great secret formulas to enhance wealth.

Example Building inside enclosed Area

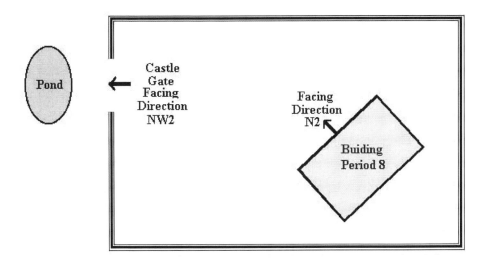

Example

Period 8 Shopping Complex

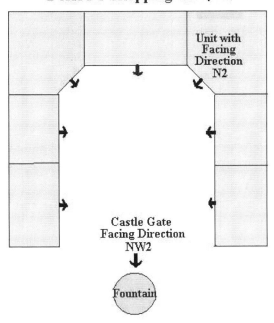

The Castle Gate Formula explains from which directions the energy, which is the most prosperous during a respective period, enters the enclosed area. In this way the building will come to enjoy the most prosperous energy of the period, which it otherwise could not.

Let us now demystify the Castle Gate Formula

What are the Castle Gates?
The Castle Gates are nothing but the most auspicious Facing Directions of a period.

Why are the Castle Gates the most auspicious Facing Directions?
The Castle Gates have the period number as Facing Star number in the Facing Palace and the Facing Stars fly descending (yin).

Example

1 4 6	6 8 2	8 6 4
9 5 5	2 -3 **7**	4 1 9
5 9 1	**7 7** 3	3 2 8

↓
Facing N 2/3

Harmony Feature of
the Combination of
Earth Base and
Facing Stars
4/6 and 6/4
8/2 and 2/8
5/5 and 5/5
3/7 and 7/3
9/1 and 1/9

Charts having Facing Stars flying descending are said to have their auspicious character enhanced when water is seen in the Facing Direction.

Further more, descending flying Facing Stars in combination with the Earth Base Stars create a harmony feature, which is very auspicious and wealth enhancing. This harmony feature is comparable to the harmony feature of the "Combination of 10 Charts".

Why has water got to be at the Castle Gate?
In all Castle Gate directions the Facing Star flies descending (yin).

This condition is said to be very auspicious, when water is seen at the Facing Direction (see chapter on Four Combinations of ascending and descending Facing and Mountain Stars).

Why do Castle Gates depend on the condition that the building is surrounded by higher structures leaving one gap open?
This condition for the Castle Gates is to ensure that there are no other directions competing as Facing Direction.

How to find out which directions in a given period qualify as Castle Gates?
Look at the Geomantic Charts for all 24 Facing Directions of a given period. Identify the Facing Directions which have the period number as Facing Star number in the Facing Palace. These Facing Directions qualify as Castle Gates.

Can the Castle Gate Formula be applied on a house surrounded by flat land or on an apartment?
Yes, in case of a house on flat land we have to select the Castle Gate direction, which is 45° apart from the Facing Direction of the building and disqualify all other directions by surrounding the building with either walls or trees and bushes. Only for apartments which have a Facing Direction independent from the Facing Direction of the building the formula could be used, if one of the possible Facing Directions of the apartment is a Castle Gate direction and could be turned into the Facing Direction by disqualifying all other directions as competing Facing Direction by means of curtains, screens or other devices.

Can we use more than one of the Castle Gate directions for one building?
This is a very tempting thought, but the formula makes it very clear that there should be only one "gap".

Geomantic Charts of Period 8

Facing Palaces, which are Castle Gates, have Facing Stars Number 8 Their Facing Stars fly descending (yin)

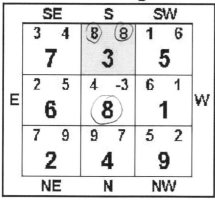

Period 8 Facing N 2/3

SE	S	SW
4 3 **7**	8 8 **3**	6 1 **5**
5 2 **6**	-3 4 **8**	1 6 **1**
9 7 **2**	7 9 **4**	2 5 **9**

E / W, NE / N / NW

Period 8 Facing N 1

SE	S	SW
2 5 **7**	7 9 **3**	9 7 **5**
1 6 **6**	3 -4 **8**	5 2 **1**
6 1 **2**	8 8 **4**	4 3 **9**

E / W, NE / N / NW

Period 8 Facing S 2/3

SE	S	SW
3 4 **7**	⑧ ⑧ **3**	1 6 **5**
2 5 **6**	4 -3 ⑧	6 1 **1**
7 9 **2**	9 7 **4**	5 2 **9**

E / W, NE / N / NW

Period 8 Facing S 1

SE	S	SW
5 2 **7**	9 7 **3**	7 9 **5**
6 1 **6**	-4 3 **8**	2 5 **1**
1 6 **2**	8 8 **4**	3 4 **9**

E / W, NE / N / NW

Period 8 Facing E 2/3

	SE	S	SW	
	2 5 **7**	6 1 **3**	4 3 **5**	
E	3 4 **6**	-1 6 **8**	8 8 **1**	**W**
	7 9 **2**	5 2 **4**	9 7 **9**	
	NE	N	NW	

Period 8 Facing E 1

	SE	S	SW	
	9 7 **7**	5 2 **3**	7 9 **5**	
E	8 8 **6**	1 -6 **8**	3 4 **1**	**W**
	4 3 **2**	6 1 **4**	2 5 **9**	
	NE	N	NW	

Period 8 Facing W 2/3

	SE	S	SW	
	5 2 **7**	1 6 **3**	3 4 **5**	
E	4 3 **6**	6 -1 **8**	8 8 **1**	**W**
	9 7 **2**	2 5 **4**	7 9 **9**	
	NE	N	NW	

Period 8 Facing W 1

	SE	S	SW	
	7 9 **7**	2 5 **3**	9 7 **5**	
E	8 8 **6**	-6 1 **8**	4 3 **1**	**W**
	3 4 **2**	1 6 **4**	5 2 **9**	
	NE	N	NW	

Period 8 Facing NE 2/3

SE	S	SW	
4 1 **7**	9 6 **3**	2 8 **5**	
E 3 9 **6**	5 2 **8**	7 4 **1**	W
8 5 **2**	1 7 **4**	6 3 **9**	
NE	N	NW	

Period 8 Facing NE 1

SE	S	SW	
6 3 **7**	1 7 **3**	8 5 **5**	
E 7 4 **6**	-5 -2 **8**	3 9 **1**	W
2 8 **2**	9 6 **4**	4 1 **9**	
NE	N	NW	

Period 8 Facing SW 2/3

SE	S	SW	
1 4 **7**	6 9 **3**	8 2 **5**	
E 9 3 **6**	2 5 **8**	4 7 **1**	W
5 8 **2**	7 1 **4**	3 6 **9**	
NE	N	NW	

Period 8 Facing SW1

SE	S	SW	
3 6 **7**	7 1 **3**	5 8 **5**	
E 4 7 **6**	-2 -5 **8**	9 3 **1**	W
8 2 **2**	6 9 **4**	1 4 **9**	
NE	N	NW	

Period 8 Facing SE 2/3

SE	S	SW	
1 8 **7**	5 3 **3**	3 1 **5**	
E	2 9 **6**	-9 -7 **8**	7 5 **1**	W
6 4 **2**	4 2 **4**	8 6 **9**	
NE	N	NW	

Period 8 Facing SE 1

SE	S	SW	
8 6 **7**	4 2 **3**	6 4 **5**	
E	7 5 **6**	9 7 **8**	2 9 **1**	W
3 1 **2**	5 3 **4**	1 8 **9**	
NE	N	NW	

Period 8 Facing NW 2/3

SE	S	SW	
8 1 **7**	3 5 **3**	1 3 **5**	
E	9 2 **6**	-7 -9 **8**	5 7 **1**	W
4 6 **2**	2 4 **4**	6 8 **9**	
NE	N	NW	

Period 8 Facing NW 1

SE	S	SW	
6 B **7**	2 4 **3**	4 6 **5**	
E	5 7 **6**	7 9 **8**	9 2 **1**	W
1 3 **2**	3 5 **4**	8 1 **9**	
NE	N	NW	

Facing Directions, which qualify as Castle Gates in Period 8

The following Facing Directions of period 8 buildings qualify as Castle Gates:
Facing Directions: **N1, NE1, E1, SE2/3, S2/3, SW1, W2/3, NW2/3,**

Castle Gates in Period 8

Facing Direction	Primary Castle Gate	Secondary Castle Gate
S1		SW1
S2	SE2	

S3	SE3	
SW1		
SW2	W2	S2
SW3	W3	S3
W1	SW1	
W2		NW2
W3		NW3
NW1	N1	
NW2		W2
NW3		W3
N1		NE1
N2	NW2	
N3	NW3	
NE1	E1	N1
NE2		
NE3		
E1	NE1	
E2		SE2
E3		SE3
SE1		E1
SE2	S2	
SE3	S3	

Two Types of Facing Directions of Buildings

1.) As most buildings, houses or apartments confirm to rectangular shapes even when corners may be missing, the Facing Direction of a building decides which of the Castle Gates can be made use of. Under the condition that the building has a rectangular shape and faces either: **N1, NE1, E1, SE1, S1, SW1, W1, NW1 we can use in the period of 8** only the Castle Gate directions: **N1, NE1, E1, and SW1.**

2.) Under the condition that the building has a rectangular shape and faces either: **N2/3, NE2/3, E2/3, SE2/3, S2/3, SW2/3, W2/3, NW2/3 we can use in the period of 8** only the Castle Gate directions: **SE2/3, S2/3, W2/3 and NW2/3.**

When Castle Gate Direction and the Facing Direction of a Building are Identical

In such a case the building has already got the most prosperous Facing Direction, which should be activated by placing a water feature in that direction. Nothing else needs to be done.

The Castle Gate Formula serves to direct into a Building the most prosperous energy of a Period, which the Building on account of its Facing Direction could otherwise not enjoy.

The Energies of the Eight Directions

Earlier Heaven   **Earlier Heaven in numbers**

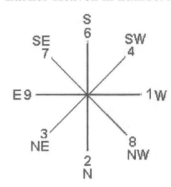

Above diagrams show the arrangement of energies of the Earlier Heaven. The blue numbers and their directions represent energies, which are predominantly yin in character and the red ones are predominantly yang.

The blue numbers stand for contraction and decay and are the malevolent energies.

The red numbers signify expansion and growth and are the benevolent energies.

Both groups of energies are clearly divided as can be observed in all cycles of change in nature.

The dividing line between both groups as in the example of the cycle of a day is according to the concept of the Taoist Cosmology not from sunrise to sunset, but from midnight to noon.

It is the factor of growth, which divides the two groups. At noon yin is born and starts growing until it reaches its peak at midnight when yang starts growing until it reaches its culmination at noon.

How to read the Stars

When assessing the energy of a palace we have to keep the followii
mind:

1. The Guest / Host relationship of the energies of the stars (see relevant chapter).

2. The interaction of the Five Elements in the relationship of the stars (see relevant chapter).

3. And last but not least the strength of the energies represented by the stars.

The Facing Star is strongest, the Earth Base Star is of intermediate strength and the Mountain has a low level of strength followed by the Annual and Monthly Stars.

When assessing the energy of a building or site we have to keep the following factors in mind:

1. The energies of the Facing Palace are, by the fact that the directional energy enters a building at this palace, the strongest.

2. The Center Palace, on account of its position, relates to all other palaces and thereby has influence on their energies. It is therefore said the energies of the Center Palace affect all residents of the building.

3. The Palace in which the main door (most used door) is located, is of special importance since the traffic through this door activates the energies of the respective palace.

The System of the 5 Elements

5 different Interactions of Energy.

These are:
1. The full and nourishing energy coming from the front.
2. The empty energy coming from behind.
3. The robbing energy coming from the undefeated.
4. The small energy coming from the defeated.
5. The direct energy coming from the same element itself

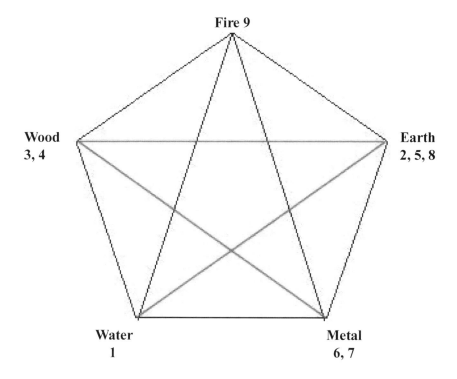

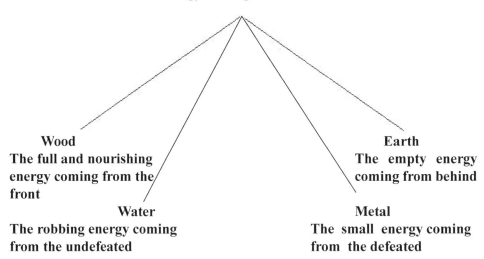

Fire
The direct energy coming from the same element

Wood
The full and nourishing
energy coming from the
front

Earth
The empty energy
coming from behind

Water
The robbing energy coming
from the undefeated

Metal
The small energy coming
from the defeated

Earth
The direct energy coming from the same element

Fire
The full and nourishing
energy coming from
the front

Metal
The empty energy
coming from
behind

Wood
The robbing energy coming
from the undefeated

Water
The small energy coming
from the defeated

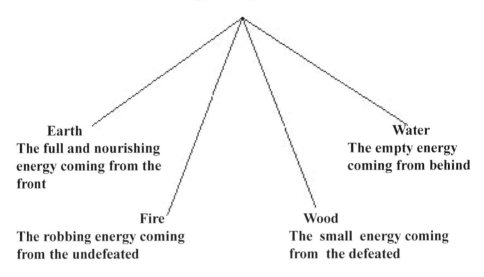

Metal
The direct energy coming from the same element

Earth
The full and nourishing
energy coming from the
front

Water
The empty energy
coming from behind

Fire
The robbing energy coming
from the undefeated

Wood
The small energy coming
from the defeated

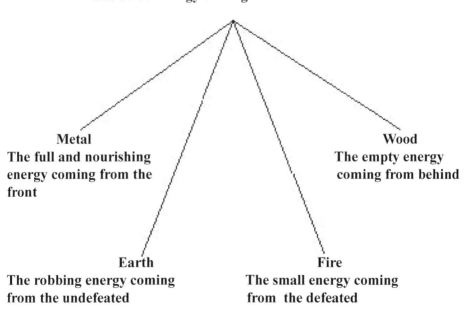

Water
The direct energy coming from the same element

Metal
The full and nourishing
energy coming from the
front

Wood
The empty energy
coming from behind

Earth
The robbing energy coming
from the undefeated

Fire
The small energy coming
from the defeated

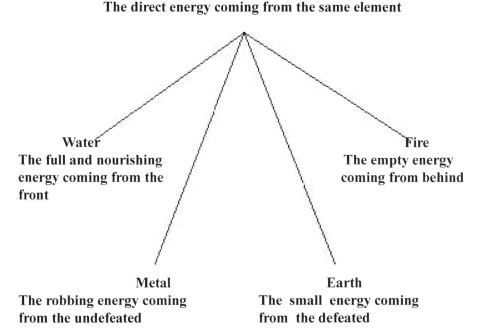

Wood
The direct energy coming from the same element

Water
The full and nourishing energy coming from the front

Fire
The empty energy coming from behind

Metal
The robbing energy coming from the undefeated

Earth
The small energy coming from the defeated

Let us now examine how the interaction of the energies works.
Supposing a palace has the Earth Base 9, Facing Star 6 and Mountain Star 4. Looking at Earth Base 9 and Facing Star 6 we could come to the conclusion the fire element of 9 destroys the metal element of the 6. We also could think the metal element of the 6 attacks the fire element of the 9.
Is the metal element of the 6 destroying the wood element of the 4 or is the wood element of the 4 effecting the metal element of the 6 ?
Is the wood element of the 4 nourishing the fire element of the 9 or is the fire element of the 9 draining the wood element of the 4 ?

Which of these possibilities is the correct one?
All are correct by themselves, as far as the interaction of the five elements are concerned. However, since the energies in a palace do not all have the same status but are acting upon each other in a fashion of Host energy and Guest energies, their interactions follow a certain pattern dictated by their status (see Host/Guest relationship of stars).
We have to find out which of the different energies interacts with any of the other ones. Is the metal energy of 6 interacting with the fire energy of 9 or is the fire of

9 interacting with the metal of 6 ? Both interactions do generally not take place under the same conditions at the same time.

1. **The Earth Base Star represents the resident or Host energy of a palace. The Facing and Mountain Stars are visiting or Guest energies and such are the Annual and the Monthly Stars, which interact first of all with the Earth Base Star, but may also with other stars (see Host / Guest relationship of the stars).**

2. **The interaction of the Facing and the Mountain Star with the Earth Base is the reason why, in the unconditional interaction of certain combinations of stars, the numbers of the Earth Base and the Facing Star cannot be exchanged.**

3. **The special effect of the combination Earth Base 8 and Facing Star 9, which stands for happy relationships, is not given in a combination of Earth Base 9 and Facing Star 8. In the first example the 9 enhances the 8, whereas in the second the 8 drains the energy of the 9.**

4. **When analyzing the interaction of the stars according to the Five Elements we must keep in mind that the interaction of the Facing Star with the Earth Base is to be seen as more important than the interaction of the Mountain Star with the Earth Base Star.**

5. **This is on account of the Facing Star being considered to carry stronger energy than the Mountain Star. The Annual and the Monthly Stars are still less powerful and their interaction is therefore considered last.**

Why should this be so is a question, which could be asked.
We know that the energy represented by the Earth Base is defined by the time factor of construction, the period of the building. The Earth Base energy is therefore a part of the building, which will not change unless structural changes are made, which change the building to an extent that it can be considered to be a new one.

Energy, which enters a building from the Facing Direction, is not a part of the building as such, as the Earth Base energy is. It is a visiting energy, which enters the building from the Facing Direction, and its quality is dependent on the Facing Direction. With changes in the Facing Direction this energy also changes. Changes in the Facing Direction can be brought about by factors which are part of the building such as installing new windows and changing doors, as well as by changes in the external environment such as the growth of trees, the construction of buildings and roads in the vicinity.

The visiting energy of the Facing and Mountain Stars are both entering the building from the Facing Direction. Both energies have to be seen as complimenting each other. They relate to each other in the same way as the two basic forces yin and yang do and represent the duality of the cosmic energy.

We also know that the Facing Direction is the direction, which has the greatest exposure to yang energy (movement, noise, light, expansion in the form of unobstructed view). The Facing Star can therefore be seen as the star that carries this strong yang energy which is complimented by the predominantly yin energy of the Mountain Star. I think this makes it obvious that the Facing Star represents energy, which is more forceful than that of the Mountain Star. Considering this, we can understand that the interaction of the Facing Star with Earth Base is the most important feature in a palace.

The Annual and the Monthly Stars are also visiting energies brought about by short time changes in the universe. They interact first of all with the Earth Base energy.

How to establish Harmony in the Interaction of Energies

Taking the example from above, the wood of Mountain Star 4 and the metal of the Facing Star 6 interact with the fire of the Earth Base.

To balance the effect the metal of Facing Star 6 has on the Earth Base 9, we have to use water as countermeasure. To understand why we use water, please look at the chart of the Five Elements. Metal relates to fire as the small energy coming from the defeated and water relates to fire as the robbing energy coming from the undefeated. These two energies have got to get balanced.

To nullify the effect wood has on fire, we should use the earth element because the full and nourishing energy coming from the front and the empty energy coming from behind have got to get balanced.

1. **As you have seen from the above example, the full and nourishing energy coming from the front and the empty energy coming from behind are opposing forces in the interaction which have to get balanced in order to establish harmony.**

2. **Similarly the robbing energy coming from the undefeated and the small energy coming from the defeated are opposing forces, which have to be harmonized.**

3. What is often called the Nourishing Cycle, where in the order of fire, earth, metal, water and wood, the elements nourish each other, is in its reverse direction of fire, wood, water, metal and earth a Draining Cycle.

4. The Destructive Cycle in the order of fire, metal, wood, earth and water in its reverse direction fire, water, earth, wood and metal is similar to the Nourishing Cycle enhancing the energies.

5. Please keep in mind that the Nourishing Cycle and the Destructive Cycle and their reverse directions do not necessarily create harmony, but give a special strengthening or weakening effect.

6. Harmony is achieved only by balancing the opposing energies as described under No. 1 and 2

Keeping our Objectives in Mind when deciding on Countermeasures and Enhancers

When considering the interaction of the elements and the countermeasures to apply, it is most important to keep our objectives in mind, which may be harmony or the stimulation or removal of certain effects.

We therefore have to consider first if the stars are benevolent or malevolent. Thereafter we see if the effect the Facing Star has on the Earth Base Star, is desirable or undesirable. The effect of the Mountain Star on the Earth Base and later the effect of the Annual and the monthly star must be considered, before we can decide on countermeasures or enhancers.

The Interaction of the Five Elements is the Basis on which to decide on Enhancers and Countermeasures

Stars having the numbers 2 and 5 are malevolent and undesirable. Number 2 in combination with other stars will mostly, but not always have bad effects. Our objective therefore is to destroy or weaken them.

Star number 9 is equally undesirable, but in certain combinations such as 8 / 9, where Earth Base is 8 and the Facing Star is 9, it is very desirable. The undesirable character of star 9 is mainly due to the fact that its fire element will enhance the strength of the malevolent stars 2 and 5, but also for its likelihood to cause damage or injury by fire if the palace in which the star 9 is found, has a fireplace such as a stove in the kitchen.

Stars having the numbers 1, 4, 6, and 8 are very desirable and so are their combinations, except for the combination 8/3 and 8/4 when number 8 is the Earth Base Star. Our objective is to enhance and nourish them. Under certain conditions to apply enhancers will be advisable. We shall see later how this is done
.

The stars 3 and 7 are considered neutral in their action, but in combination with other stars can at times be benevolent or very destructive and countermeasures have to be applied to cure their effect.

The Host / Guest Relationship of the Stars

Different schools use different methods depending on which of the 3 stars, the Facing, the Mountain or the Earth Base Star is seen as more important. Generally speaking two systems are in use:

1. **System 1 pays first of all attention to the yin/yang duality of the building** represented by the Mountain and Facing Stars and therefore considers their interaction as most important. The energy of the Earth Base Star is understood to be of secondary importance.

2. **System 2 considers primarily the level of energy** of the stars and therefore concentrates on the interaction of the Facing and the Earth Base Stars, since these two stars are seen as representing the strongest energies, which cause the greatest affect on the occupants well-being. The Mountain Star is considered to have a low level of energy but is taken into account as well.

Both systems do sometimes take also the Later Heaven arrangement of energies into account when analyzing the interaction of the stars.

The Interaction of the Stars in different Palaces

Both systems give greatest importance to the Facing Palace, as directional energy enters a building at the Facing Palace and from there is channeled to the rest of the building, influencing the energies in all other palaces to some extent. The energies present in the Facing Palace are therefore understood to be dominant.
Apart from the interaction of the stars in the Facing Palace the two systems are different in the evaluation of energies in the rest of the palaces.

1. **System 1** which holds the view that the interaction of the Facing and Mountain Star is most important pays equal attention to their interaction in the Facing and the Sitting Palace. These two Palaces are seen as representing the same yin/yang duality attributed to the two stars.
    They generally see a need for the period's Mountain and Facing Star in these two palaces to be supported by external features, such as mountains or tall structures for Mountain Stars and water features or roads for Facing Stars, which are believed to activate the respective stars.

Thereafter the Mountain and Facing Stars of the other 7 palaces are analyzed in their Host/Guest relationship. Their support by external features is understood to be essential.

2. System 2, which gives more importance to the Facing and the Earth Base Stars, while seeing the interaction of the Stars in the Facing Palace as most important, pays equal attention to the interaction of the stars in all the other Palaces. The presence of external features in the directions of the Facing or Mountain Stars is not seen as a compelling influence. The harmony features of the energies in the palaces are on the other hand seen as very important (see The Four Combinations of Facing and Mountain Stars flying either ascending or descending).

Both systems pay special attention to the interaction of the stars in the palace in which the main door is located.
The Centre Palace too receives special attention, since its energies are said to affect all residents of the building.

Example of Host / Guest Relationships of both Systems

Period 7 Building

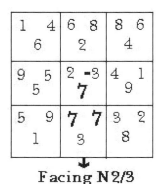

Facing N 2/3

Facing Palace

Guest 7	Host 7
3	

All 9 Palaces

Sitting Palace

Host 6	Guest 8
2	

Guest	Guest
Host	

Guest
Period Earth Base Stars

6	2	4
5	7	9
1	3	8

Host
Later Heaven Stars

4	9	2
3	5	7
8	1	6

The Host / Guest Relationship of the Stars

Auspicious Relationships

When the Guest enhances the Host =   It is the full and nourishing energy coming from the front

When the Guest and the Host are the same =   The direct energy coming from the same element

| When the Host is against the Guest = | It is the small energy coming from the defeated |

Inauspicious Relationships

| When the Host enhances the Guest = | It is the empty energy coming from behind |

| When the Guest is against the Host = | It is the robbing energy coming from the undefeated |

The Host / Guest Relationship in the Interaction of the Five Elements

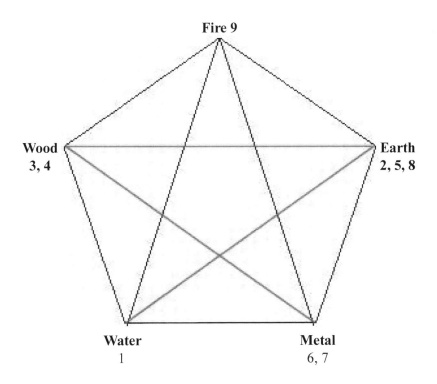

Host

Water
The direct energy coming from the same element

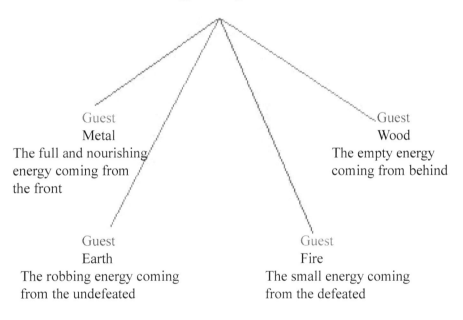

Guest
Metal
The full and nourishing
energy coming from
the front

Guest
Wood
The empty energy
coming from behind

Guest
Earth
The robbing energy coming
from the undefeated

Guest
Fire
The small energy coming
from the defeated

Host

Wood
The direct energy coming from the same element

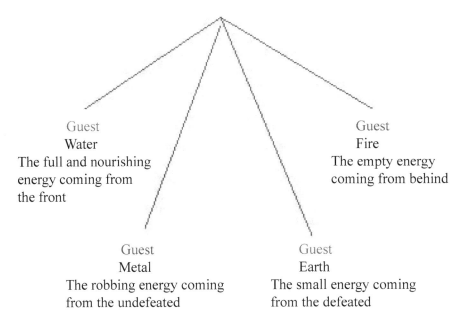

Guest
Water
The full and nourishing
energy coming from
the front

Guest
Fire
The empty energy
coming from behind

Guest
Metal
The robbing energy coming
from the undefeated

Guest
Earth
The small energy coming
from the defeated

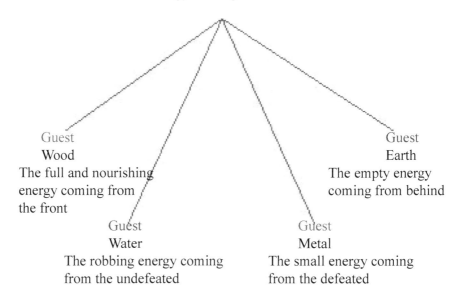

Host

Fire
The direct energy coming from the same element

Guest
Wood
The full and nourishing
energy coming from
the front

Guest
Earth
The empty energy
coming from behind

Guest
Water
The robbing energy coming
from the undefeated

Guest
Metal
The small energy coming
from the defeated

Host

Earth
The direct energy coming from the same element

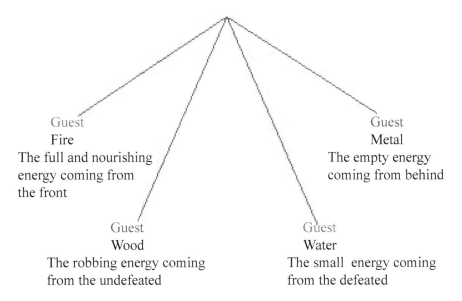

Guest
Fire
The full and nourishing
energy coming from
the front

Guest
Metal
The empty energy
coming from behind

Guest
Wood
The robbing energy coming
from the undefeated

Guest
Water
The small energy coming
from the defeated

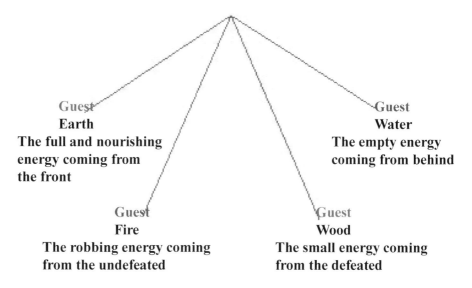

Host

Metal
The direct energy coming from the same element

Guest
Earth
The full and nourishing energy coming from the front

Guest
Water
The empty energy coming from behind

Guest
Fire
The robbing energy coming from the undefeated

Guest
Wood
The small energy coming from the defeated

Example of System 1 for a Period 7 Building Facing N2/3

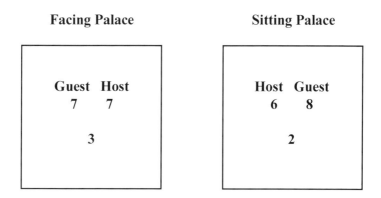

Facing Palace

Guest	Host
7	7

3

Sitting Palace

Host	Guest
6	8

2

Facing Palace: When the Guest and the Host are the same, the relationship is auspicious.

The energy of the Host is reinforced by the energy of the Guest. Since the Host is the Facing Star, this energy combination is good for wealth but only in the period 7 when its energy is timely. In period 8 when the energy is not timely anymore, the combination will cause armed robbery, loss and conflicts.

Remedies: To remove the double 7, which is malevolent in period 8 we should make use of water, which will weaken their metal element energy.

Sitting Palace: When the Guest enhances the Host the relationship is auspicious. The energy of the Host is enhanced by the full and nourishing energy of the Guest coming from the front.

Since the Host is the Sitting Star, this energy combination is good for human relationships and health. Further more the combination of 6 and 8 is understood to give success in financial and other competitive ventures.

Example of System 2 for a Period 7 Building Facing N 2/3

All 9 Palaces

All 9 Palaces

Guest 7 Guest 7 Host 3	Guest 6 Guest 8 Host 2

Facing Palace: When the Guest is against the Host, it is the robbing energy coming from the undefeated Guest, which will destroy the energy of the Host. This relationship is inauspicious and will cause armed robbery, loss and conflicts.

Remedies: The earth element is to be used as countermeasure to cure the negative effect. A boulder or small stones, representing the Earth Element number 8, will balance the affect, which the metal element of the 7 has on the wood element of the 3 and will combine with the metal element of the 7 to perfect harmony of yin and yang (see harmony features of the two Heavens).

Sitting Palace: When the Guest (Facing Star 8) is acting on the Host (Earth Base 2) the effect is neither depleting nor enhancing, but reinforcing the energy of the Host. Since the Facing Star is stronger than the Earth Base Star benevolent energy of the Facing Star will conquer the malevolent energy of the Earth Base Star.

The Guest (Mountain Star 6), when acting on the Host (Earth Base Star 2), is the empty energy coming from behind draining the energy of the Host, but also combining with the energy of the Host (Earth Base 2) and thereby creating perfect harmony of yin and yang (see harmony feature of the Earlier Heaven).

We can conclude that the energies in the Sitting Palace will greatly support the growth of wealth and the occupants will be respected and will succeed in their endeavors.

Assessing the Energy of the Stars in a Palace We should always remember

Facing Star can be Host or Guest to the Mountain Star.
The Mountain Star can be Host or Guest to the Facing Star.

In other words this means that the Facing Star can act on the Mountain Star and the Mountain Star can act on the Facing Star.

The Facing Star can only be Guests to the Earth Base Star.
The Mountain Star can only be Guests to the Earth Base Star

This means that the Facing Star acts on the Earth Base Star, but the Earth Base Star does not act on the Facing Star and the Mountain Star acts on the Earth Base Star, but the Earth Base Star does not act on the Mountain Star.

The Annual Stars are Guests to
the Earth Base, the Mountain and the Facing Stars

The Annual Stars act on the Earth Base Star. The Earth Base Star does not act on the Annual Stars. The Annual Stars act on the Facing and the Mountain Stars. The Facing and the Mountain Stars do not act on the Annual Stars.

The Monthly Stars are Guests to the Annual Stars
the Earth Base, the Facing and the Mountain Stars

The Monthly Stars act on the Annual Stars. The Annual Stars do not act on the Monthly Stars. Mountain Stars. The Earth Base, the Facing and the Mountain Stars do not act on the Monthly Stars.

Countermeasures and Enhancers are Guest Energies

Countermeasures and enhancers are Guest Energies. They act on the Earth Base, the Facing, the Mountain, the Annual and the Monthly Stars as well as on each other.

The most Auspicious Relationship of the Stars

The Facing Star and the Mountain Star enhance the Earth Base Star and the Earth Base Star enhances the Later Heaven Star.

Example
Period 6 Building Facing NE 1

NE Palace

6	3
9	

Later Heaven

4	9	2
3	5	7
8	1	6

Facing Star (Guest) is the full and nourishing energy coming from the front enhancing the Earth Base Star (Host).

The Mountain Star (Guest) is the small energy coming from the defeated helping the Earth Base Star (Host).

The Earth Base Star (Guest) is the full and nourishing energy coming from the front enhancing the Later Heaven Star (Host).

The most Inauspicious Relationship of the Stars

The Facing and the Mountain Star are against the Earth Base Star and the Earth Base Star is against the Later Heaven Star.

Example
Period 3 Building Facing S1

N Palace

3	3
8	

Later Heaven

4	9	2
3	5	7
8	1	6

Facing and Sitting Star (Guests) are the robbing energy coming from the undefeated destroying the Earth Base Star (Host).

Earth Base Star (Guest) is the robbing energy coming from the undefeated destroying the Later Heaven Star (Host).

.

The Use of Color in Feng Shui

Almost every modern book on Feng Shui advises to use colors to stimulate certain attributes of the four cardinal and the four secondary   compass directions.

Since there is obviously some confusion regarding the use of colors in Feng Shui the following may bring better understanding of the matter.

According to the System of the Five Elements

1. The Wood Element is the domain of color
2. The Fire Element is the domain of odor
3. The Metal Element is the domain of sound
4. The Water Element is the domain of flowing, moving liquids.
5. The Earth Element is the domain of flavor

The System of the Five Elements knows

1. Five colors
2. Five odors
3. Five sounds
4. Five ways of liquids in motion
5. Five different flavors

Being concerned with the effectiveness of the use of color in Feng Shui we should analyze their use in the interaction of the Five Elements.
The five colors: red, yellow, green, white and blackish blue are manifestations of the Wood Element

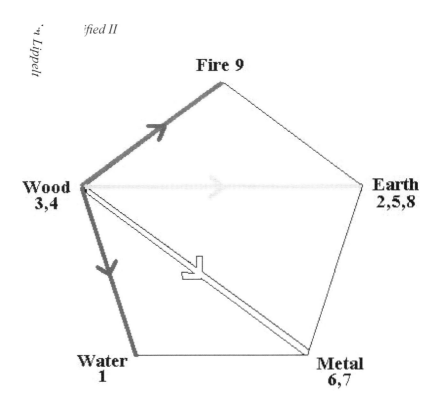

Fire 9

Wood
3,4

Earth
2,5,8

Water
1

Metal
6,7

1. Green is a manifestation of the Wood Element in its own element.
2. Red is a manifestation of the Wood Element in its interaction with the Fire Element and thereby nourishing and enhancing it.
3. Yellow is a manifestation of the Wood Element in its interaction with the Earth Element and thereby destroying it.
4. Blackish blue is a manifestation of the Wood Element in its interaction with the Water Element and thereby draining it.
5. White is a manifestation of the Wood Element in its interaction with the Metal Element and thereby helping it.

From the above we can understand that

1. In Feng Shui red is the most effective color since it represents an energy, which nourishes and enhances the Fire Element.
2. White can also be used since it helps the Metal Element, especially when the presence of the Fire Element (star combination 6 / 9 and 7/9) threatens to destroy it.
3. Yellow could also be used since it destroys the Earth Element. The strange sounding recommendation by some masters to appease the stars 2 and 5 with their own element color yellow is after all not so strange, but has its

value since yellow will destroy the Earth Element of the stars 2 and using yellow we may however end up creating a star combination ⌐ ⌐ ⌐, which as all of us know, is not desirable.

4. Green can be used to reinforce the Wood Element, but there is little to gain by it.
5. Blackish blue should never be used since it drains the Water Element.

The Color Red

Of the five colors representing the interaction of the Wood Element with the Five Elements, it is only the color red, which brings effective results when used in Feng Shui. Red will enhance the Earth Element (the stars 2, 5 and 8). The color red will give great results in combination with star 8, but must strictly be avoided when the stars 2 and 5 are present.

Using the Color Red as a General Enhancer

In the Chinese tradition the color red is a symbol of prosperity and happiness. It is therefore not surprising that the color red is used as a general enhancer when the Earth Base and the Facing and Mountain Stars in a palace are benevolent in nature.

The color red, which represents the fire element, is thought to enhance the auspicious effect of the benevolent stars 1, 4, 6 and 8. The condition for using red as a general enhancer is that all the stars in a palace are benevolent.

The color red should never be used when stars number 2, 5 and 9 are present in the palace and when a fireplace is located there.

Using the color red, as a general enhancer under the a.m. conditions is a time honored method based on the experiences of innumerable generations of certain schools.

Lineage holders of these schools may not always be in a position to explain the rational of the method. To many of them it is a method, which they use, but with out knowing how it works. Tradition has many examples for this. Knowledge is often handed over like a tool enabling the student to use it without actually knowing why and how it works.

Let us attempt to understand if and why and how this method works by analyzing it on the basis of the interaction of the Five Elements.

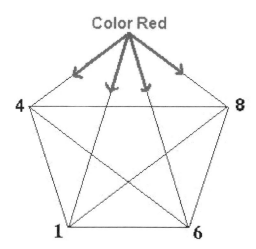

As you see in the above diagram the four benevolent stars represent four of the elements. To make it the complete Five Elements the fire element would have to be added.

When Earth Base, the Facing, the Mountain and the Annual Star all have benevolent numbers, you complete the interaction of the Five Elements by using the color red as a general enhancer.

If only the Earth Base, the Facing and the Mountain Star have benevolent numbers and the number of the Annual Star is neither 2, 5 or 9, the color red as general enhancer can be used with benefit under certain conditions only.

Considering the interaction of the Earth Base, the Facing and the Mountain star, all having benevolent numbers, 24 combinations are possible (see under interaction of benevolent stars).

Out of this 24 star combinations 6 combinations (1/8/4, 4/8/1, 1/8/6, 6/8/1, 6/1/8, 8/1/6) will rightly benefit from the color red as an enhancer (see under interaction of benevolent stars).

A further 12 combinations (1/6/4, 4/6/1, 4/6/8, 8/6/4, 1/4/8, 8/4/1, 4/8/6, 6/8/4, 4/1/8, 8/1/4, 6/4/1, 1/4/6) will also benefit if the color red is used as an enhancer to establish harmony (see under interaction of benevolent stars).

The combinations (1/6/4, 4/6/1, 4/8/6, 6/8/4, 4/1/8, 8/1/4, 6/4/1, 1/4/6) would benefit, but in addition to the color red, another element enhancer should be used to develop their full potential (see under interaction of benevolent stars).

The combinations (6/1/4, 4/1/6) will benefit, if the color red were used as an enhancer, since it would strengthen the Earth Base, but it will disturb the harmony.

The combinations (1/6/8, 8/6/1, 6/4/8, 8/4/6) will not benefit from the color red as a general enhancer but will be harmed by it.

As we have seen from the above, the method of using the color red as a general enhancer, when all three stars in a palace are benevolent, has its value and is correct in 75% of all possible combinations of benevolent stars. This ensures a very high rate of success when applied. Real harm can be caused only in 16.66% of all possible cases.

This method is therefore suitable to be used by those who do not know how to apply the interaction of the Five Elements in order to understand the energies of a palace and to decide on enhancers and countermeasures.

However, for those who feel confident that they are able to apply the interaction of the Five Elements this method may not have any attraction.

The Four Combinations of Mountain and Facing Stars

The Four Combinations:

- The Mountain Star is flying yin (descending) and the Facing Star is flying yang (ascending).
- The Mountain Star is flying yang (ascending) and the Facing Star is flying yang (ascending).
- The Mountain Star is flying yang (ascending) and the Facing Star is flying yin (descending).
- The Mountain Star is flying yin (descending) and the Facing Star is flying yin (descending).

All Geomantic Charts for the 24 Compass Directions (mountains) of the 9 Periods have one of these Four Combinations.

Mountain Star yang Facing Star yin

9 5 6	5 9 2	7 7 4
8 6 5	1 -4 7	3 2 9
4 1 1	6 8 3	2 3 8

Mountain Star yang Facing Star yang

9 3 6	5 8 2	7 1 4
8 2 5	1 4 7	3 6 9
4 7 1	6 9 3	2 5 8

Mountain Star yin Facing Star yin

2 5 6	6 9 2	4 7 4
3 6 5	-1 -4 7	8 2 9
7 1 1	5 8 3	9 3 8

Mountain Star yin Facing Star yang

2 3 6	6 8 2	4 1 4
3 2 5	-1 4 7	8 6 9
7 7 1	5 9 3	9 5 8

Two Systems of Interpretation based on Different Concepts.

The four Sequent Combinations are taken into account by all schools. They are a very basic and integral part of Flying Star Feng Shui.

System 1

System 1 is based on harmony features of energy caused by the descending (yin) way the stars are flying in the chart. The presence of environmental structures to support the Facing and/or Mountain Star are not recognized to be essential.

Ascending Mountain / Descending Facing.
If the Facing Star is flying (yin) in a descending way and is placed in the Facing Palace, the presence of water in front will greatly enhance the auspicious character of that chart.

Descending Mountain / Ascending Facing.
If the Mountain Star is flying (yin) in a descending way and is placed in the Sitting Palace, the presence of a mountain at the back will greatly enhance the auspicious character of the chart.

Ascending Mountain / Ascending Facing.
If both the Facing and the Mountain Star are flying (yang) in an ascending way, the chart will be auspicious to some extent only if there is water in front and a mountain at the back.
A chart with this condition is the least auspicious one, since both the stars are flying (yang) in an ascending way. Water in front and a mountain at the back will however give it some boost.

Descending Mountain / Descending Facing.
If both the Facing and the Mountain Star are flying (yin) in a descending way and each of them is placed in either the Sitting Palace or the Facing Palace, the chart is fortunate irrespective of any water or mountain in the Facing or Sitting Direction. This is the most fortunate of the four charts.

Having the Facing and the Mountain Star flying (yin) in a descending manner makes it extremely fortunate so that a mountain or water in either the front or back are not of much consequence.

System 2

System 2 is based on the concept that the presences of environmental structures to support the Facing and/or Mountain Star in the Facing or Sitting Palace are essential. It doesn't recognize any harmony features.

Schools which in their analysis of a chart mainly concentrate on the combination of Mountain and Facing Stars teach that the period number Facing and Mountain Stars must be timely and should be supported by appropriate features in the external environment by water and mountains for the chart to get activated.

Ascending Mountain / Descending Facing. When the timely Facing and Mountain star are placed in the Facing Palace there should be water and a mountain in front.

Descending Mountain / Ascending Facing. When the timely Facing and Mountain Star are placed in the Sitting Palace there should be water and a mountain at the back.

Ascending Mountain / Ascending Facing. When the timely Facing Star is in the Sitting Palace and the timely Mountain Star is in the Facing Palace there should be a mountain in front and water at the back.

Descending Mountain / Descending Facing. When the timely Facing Star is in the Facing Palace and the timely Mountain Star is in the sitting Palace there should be water in front and a mountain at the back.

If the environmental support of a mountain and water is given, the Facing and Mountain Star will get activated and will give finances and career as well as relationships and health luck.

If only the Facing Star is supported by water in the external environment the occupants will experience wealth and career luck.

If only the Mountain Star is supported in the external environment, the occupants will enjoy good health and good relationships.

Comparing System 1 with System 2

Example
Ascending Mountain / Descending Facing.

1 4 6 8	8 6
6	2	4

1 4	6 8	8 6
6	2	4
9 5	2 -3	4 1
5	**7**	9
5 9	**7 7**	3 2
1	3	8

↓
Facing N 2/3

System 1 is not depending on the environmental support since it recognizes harmony features in the chart, which are similar to some extent to those of the Combination of Ten Charts (see Special Charts). Water in front will, however, enhance the auspicious character of the chart since the Facing Star in the Facing Palace is flying in a descending way.

System 2: For the auspicious character of the chart to get activated a mountain and water in front are essential, since the timely Mountain and Facing Star are placed in the Facing Palace.

Example
Descending Mountain / Ascending Facing.

3 2	**7 7**	5 9
6	2	4
4 1	-2 3	9 5
5	**7**	9
8 6	6 8	1 4
1	3	8

↓
Facing N 1

System 1 is not dependent on the environmental support since it recognizes harmony features in the chart. The descending (yin) flying Mountain Star in the Sitting Palace is auspicious and the chart will be enhanced if a mountain is at the back.

System 2: Both timely stars are in the Sitting Palace. For the auspicious character of the chart to get activated, a mountain and water at the back are essential.

Example
Ascending Mountain / Ascending Facing.

Facing El◄

8 4	4 9	6 2
6	2	4
7 3	9 5	2 **7**
5	**7**	9
3 8	5 1	1 6
1	3	8

System 1 does not recognise any harmony features at all in this chart. The ascending (yang) flying Mountain Star in the Facing Palace and the ascending flying Facing Star in the Sitting Palace are not considered auspicious, but the chart will be enhanced to some extent if water is in front and a mountain at the back.

System 2: It is essential that the timely Facing Star in the Sitting Palace should be supported by water at the back and the timely Mountain Star in the Facing Palace by a mountain in front.

Example
Descending Mountain / Descending Facing.

1 6 6	5 1 2	3 8 4
2 **7** 5	-9 -5 **7**	**7** 3 9
6 2 1	4 9 3	8 4 8

Facing E 2/3 ◄

System 1 is not dependent on any environmental support since it recognises excellent harmony features which make this chart the most auspicious of the four charts, because both stars fly (yin) in a descending way. The chart is auspicious irrespective of any mountain or water at the back or in front.

System 2: The timely Mountain Star in the Sitting Palace should be supported by a mountain at the back and the timely Facing Star in the Facing Palace should be supported by water in front to activate the auspicious character of the chart

The Method of System 1

The method of system 1 needs further examination to be understood. It is based on the descending (yin) way the stars are flying in the chart, which creates harmony features of the energies of Earth Base and the descending flying Mountain and / or Facing Star.

The Harmony Feature of Perfect Balance of Number Combinations

When looking at the **Descending Mountain / Descending Facing** Chart which is period 7 Facing E 2/3, the Mountain and the Facing Star are flying (yin) descending.

The energy of the Earth Base and the descending flying Facing Star, as well as the descending flying Mountain Star make reverse energy combinations in each Palace of the chart and thereby create balance and harmony of all energies (see also Special Charts).

The Combination of Earth Base And Mountain Stars	The Combination of Earth Base And Facing Stars
1/6 and 6/1	6/6 and 6/6
5/2 and 2/5	1/2 and 2/1
3/4 and 4/3	8/4 and 4/8
9/7 and 7/9	7/5 and 5/7
8/8 and 8/8	3/9 and 9/3

This harmony feature as you can see from the above charts is found in the **Descending Mountain / Descending Facing** condition with the Mountain and the Facing Star and is therefore considered the most auspicious chart.
Ascending Mountain / Ascending Facing condition does not have this harmony feature at all and is therefore considered not auspicious.
Descending Mountain / Ascending Facing condition has the harmony feature of Earth Base with the Mountain Star.
Ascending Mountain / Descending Facing condition has the harmony feature of Earth Base with the Facing Star.

As these harmony features have to be complete to create a balance of the energies involved, they are effective only when all 9 palaces are covered by the floor plan. If a palace is missing the balance of the energies is not complete (see also Special Charts).

The Method of System 2

Method 2 is straightforward, easy to understand and makes sense. The supporting environmental features of a mountain and water have to be in the direction of the timely Mountain and Facing Star to activate the chart.

Facing Direction Requirements

However, applying this method of interpretation to a house which has e.g. an Ascending Mountain / Ascending Facing Chart, the house would have to have higher lying ground in the Facing Direction in front and water in the Sitting Direction at the back. This is simply not possible considering the requirements for Facing Directions.

Yin / Yang Duality

The Mountain and the Facing Star in a palace represent the yin / yang duality of energies. The Facing Star acts and behaves in a yang fashion and is activated by yang factors such as activity and especially by the presence of running water.

It is well known when activating a Facing Star with a water feature the Mountain Star gets depleted. This is generally put as the Mountain Star falling into the water and is due to the complementary waxing and waning of yin and yang. When yang expands yin retracts and vice versa. Activating the Facing Star the Mountain Star gets depleted and vice versa.

Having a mountain and water in front of the Facing Direction or Sitting Direction for the timely Mountain and Facing Star to get activated as claimed necessary for the **Descending Mountain / Ascending Facing** and the **Ascending Mountain / Descending Facing chart** doesn't therefore make any sense considering the yin / yang duality of both stars. Activating both stars at the same time is not possible.

The failure to realize the auspiciousness of the Descending Mountain / Descending Facing chart is generally blamed on the absence of correct supporting environmental features. Investigating, we will find that the respective buildings had "missing corners", i.e. one or more palaces are missing in the floor plan.

No doubt, the features in the external environment have an influence on the global directional energies in their vicinity. Such also has the location of entrances and the positioning of furniture in the microcosm of a building. These influences however are not of primary importance.

The influence of time (period of construction) and Facing Direction (directional exposure) of a building, which changes the global directional energies into the individual energies of a building as seen in the building's geomantic chart, is by far the most important one and harmony features of the individual energies of a building are therefore the most auspicious features of all.

Harmony Features of the Earlier and Later Heaven Arrangement of Energies

**Earlier Heaven
Arrangement of Energies**

**Later Heaven
Arrangement of Energies**

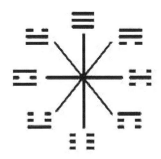

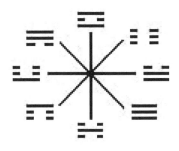

**Earlier Heaven
in numbers**

**Later Heaven
in numbers**

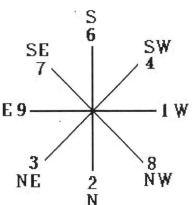

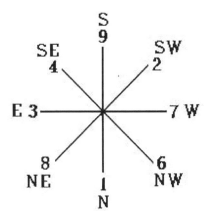

In the energy arrangement of the Earlier Heaven the opposing compass directions always give a perfectly balanced combination of three yin and three yang lines. It is therefore said that the Earlier Heaven arrangement is absolute perfect harmony of all yin and yang forces in stillness and represents the underlying reality of creation.

The energy arrangement of the Later Heaven is the actuality of energies in our world of constant change. Here the opposite compass directions always add up to a sum of ten representing a high degree of conditioned harmony.

Both harmony features are recognized in Flying Star Feng Shui. Each combination of the Earlier Heaven harmony feature is a most auspicious energy combination. The combinations of the Later Heaven harmony features are auspicious under certain conditions only.

Earlier Heaven Combinations of opposite compass directions	Later Heaven Combinations of opposite compass directions
6/2	4/6
1/9	3/7
8/7	1/9
3/4	2/8
	(5/5)

The number 5 being in the center does not have an opposing direction, but belonging to the earth element, has to be seen in line with the 2 / 8 numbers being earth element as well and all three numbers can therefore be seen as representing the NE -- SW duality of the Later Heaven.

Special Charts
The Three-Combination Chart

This is a chart having special combinations of three numbers in each of the 9 palaces. Each combination is made up of numbers of the Upper, Middle and Lower Eras and are therefore said to receive energy from all three Eras.

Upper Era consists of the Periods 1, 2, 3
Middle Era consists of the Periods 4, 5, 6
Lower Era consists of the Periods 7, 8, 9

The star combinations of Earth Base, Facing and Mountain Stars in each of the 9 Palaces of Three Combination Charts are:

1, 4, 7 / **2, 5, 8** / 3, 6, 9

and are said to represent perfect harmony of all energies of the chart.

Example of a Three-Combination Chart

Period 2 Flying Star for SW 2/3 Facing

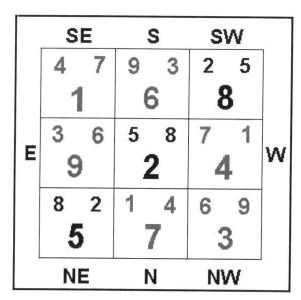

Comparing the above you can see that the number combinations in the 9 palaces of the Three Combination Charts according to the Later Heaven Arrangement of opposing directions represent harmony of the energies of each palace with those of another one.

The combination 1/4/7 is in harmony with the combination 9/6/3
The combination 7/1/4 is in harmony with the combination 3/9/6
The combination 4/7/1 is in harmony with the combination 6/3/9
The combination 2/5/8 is in harmony with the combination 8/5/2,
5/8/2 and 8/2/5

Since the Three Combination Chart involves the whole energy of each palace represented by the Earth Base, Facing and Mountain Stars, the harmony of the energies is considered complete and lasting in its benevolent effect on all aspects of human life throughout the 9 cycles. According to the waxing and waning of the strength of the energy of the Earth Base Star the benevolent effect of the Three Combination Chart is modified during the nine cycles, but never the less always present.

The perfect harmony of the Three Combination Chart is not given, when one palace and therefore one of the combinations is missing in the floor plan. The special effect of the chart will then be lost and the chart has to be treated like an ordinary one. In such case the reader is strongly advised to take care of the 2/5/8 star combinations.

The Three Combination Charts which are very auspicious in supporting good health, excellent relationships, wealth, respect and fame, are found in the Periods and Facing Directions listed below:

Period 2, Facing Direction SW 2 / 3 and Facing Direction NE 2 / 3
Period 4, Facing Direction NE 1 and Facing Direction SW 1
Period 5, Facing Direction NE 2 / 3 and Facing Direction SW 2 / 3
Period 6, Facing Direction SW 1 and Facing Direction NE 1
Period 8, Facing Direction SW 2 / 3 and Facing Direction NE 2 / 3

All in all there are 16 occurrences in 180 years.

Combination of Ten Charts

The Combination of Ten is a very high degree of harmony created by two stars only. It can be the combination of the Earth Base and Facing Stars or the combination of the Earth Base and Mountain Stars.

Later Heaven Harmony Feature
The Combination of Ten Charts are based on the Later Heaven Harmony Feature of opposing compass directions in which the numbers are always adding up to make a sum of ten.

Harmony Feature of Perfect Balance of Number Combinations.
The Combination of Ten charts have still another Harmony Feature. Each of these number combinations has in the same chart a perfect counterpart in a reversed combination such as e.g. 9/1 and 1/9 or 2/8 and 8/2.
These two features assure a high degree of balance of the energies in the Combination of Ten Charts.

Example of Combination of Ten Chart

Period 7 Facing N 2/3

	SE	S	SW	
	1　4 **6**	6　8 **2**	8　6 **4**	
E	9　5 **5**	2　-3 **7**	4　1 **9**	**W**
	5　9 **1**	7　7 **3**	3　2 **8**	
	NE	N	NW	

The above example is a Combination of Ten made up by the Earth Base and the Facing Stars. All the Star combinations come in reverse pairs.

The Reverse Pairs are:
6/4 and 4/6
2/8 and 8/2
7/3 and 3/7
1/9 and 9/1
and 5/5, which is reversible in itself

As the harmony of energies in the chart is not given in case one palace and thereby one of the star combinations is missing, the special overall auspicious effect of the Combination of Ten chart is lost and the chart has to be treated like an ordinary one. In such a case the reader is strongly advised to take care of the 5/5 combination.

Since the combinations are not based on all three stars present in each palace, they do not represent the all-round luck of the Three Combination Chart, but depending on the combination, involving either the Facing or the Mountain Stars, are said to enhance the wealth and career aspects or the good relations aspect and health of the residents.

The auspicious effect of the Combination of Ten charts is lasting through all periods because the combinations involve stars having numbers of all periods. The effect of the chart will however be modified due to the waxing and waning of the Earth Base energy in different periods.

The Combination of Ten Charts are found in the Periods and Facing Directions listed below:

Period 1, Facing Direction SE 2 / 3 and Facing Direction NW 2 / 3
Period 2, Facing Direction NE 1 and Facing Direction SW 1
Period 3, Facing Direction N 2 / 3 and Facing Direction S 2 / 3
Period 4, Facing Direction W 1 and Facing Direction E 1
Period 6, Facing Direction W 1 and Facing Direction E 1
Period 7, Facing Direction N 2 / 3 and Facing Direction S 2 / 3
Period 8, Facing Direction SW 1 and Facing Direction NE 1
Period 9, Facing Direction SE 2 / 3 and Facing Direction NW 2 / 3

All in all there are 24 occurrences in 180 years.

The Pearl String Chart

When the three stars in all 9 palaces have numbers, which connect in an unbroken sequence such as e.g. 1, 2, 3 or 8, 9, 1 it is said to be a Pearl String Chart and is supposedly very auspicious. Let us have a look to see what it is all about.

Pearl String Charts are found in the Periods and Facing Directions listed below:

Period 2, Facing Direction NW1 and SE1
Period 3, Facing Direction NW 2/3 and SE 2/3
Period 5, Facing Direction NW 2/3 and SE 2/3
Period 7, Facing Direction NW 2/3 and SE 2/3
Period 8, Facing Direction NW 1 and SE 1

While the number combinations of all the Pearl String Combination Charts are the same, they are placed in different Palaces depending on the periods and Facing Directions of the charts.

Example of a Pearl String Chart

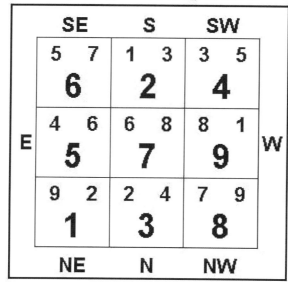

The number combinations in the 9 Palaces of all the Pearl String Combination are:

8/9/1   9 / 1 is perfect harmony of yin and yang
9/1/2   9 / 1 is perfect harmony of yin and yang
1/2/3   no harmony feature
2/3/4   3 / 4 is perfect harmony of yin and yang
3/4/5   3 / 4 is perfect harmony of yin and yang
4/5/6   4 / 6 is harmony of the opposing directions of the Later
         Heaven arrangements
5/6/7   no harmony feature
6/7/8   7 / 8 is perfect harmony of yin and yang
7/8/9   7 / 8 is perfect harmony of yin and yang

As we can see from the above only 6 of the 9 palaces have the perfect harmony, but in some palaces it is given by the combination of the Earth Base and Facing Star and in other palaces by the Earth Base and Mountain Star. In addition 1 palace has the relative harmony, which we have in the Combination of 10 Charts, and 2 palaces have no harmony feature at all.

It is doubtful that the incomplete harmony of the Pearl String Charts has any positive effect. Considering our findings above, I would not place much confidence in the auspicious character of the Pearl String Charts.

Seven Star Robbery Chart

Seven Star Robbery is a highly controversial method to be grouped under Special Charts such as the Ten Combination Chart, the Pearl String Chart and the Three Combinations Chart. The method is used to identify the potential of a building to receive not only the timely strong energy of its own period, but that of other periods as well. To make this possible the formation of so-called Parent Trigrams in the chart is the decisive factor.

The Seven Star Robbery Formation, which is causing a lot of confusion among Feng Shui practitioners, is understood in three different ways. The variations of understanding the formations are:

1. Double Period Star in the Facing Palace matching with the S Palace. These formations are found in charts of the following periods and Facing Directions:
   Period 1, facing E 1, S 2/3 and NW 1
   Period 2, facing E 2/3 and S 1
   Period 3, facing S 2/3
   Period 4, facing S 1 and NW 1
   Period 6, facing S 2/3 and NW 2/3 (Fan Fu Yin)
   Period 7, facing S 1
   Period 8, facing S 2/3 and E 1
   Period 9, facing E 2/3, NW 2/3 and S 1 (Fan Fu Yin)

2. Double Period Star in the Facing Palace matching with the N Palace. These formations are found in charts of the following Periods and Facing Directions:
   Period 1, facing W 2/3, SE 2/3, N 1 (Fan Fu Yin)
   Period 2, facing N 2/3, W 1
   Period 3, facing N 1
   Period 4, facing N 2/3, SE 2/3 (Fan Fu Yin)
   Period 6, facing SE 1, N 1
   Period 7, facing N 2/3
   Period 8, facing W 2/3, N 1
   Period 9, facing N 2/3, SE 1, W 1

3. Double Period Star in either the Facing or the Sitting Palace and a Facing Star with the number of the next period in either the Facing or the Sitting Palace.

105

Such formations are only found in the Facing Directions N 1 and N 2/3 in all periods except in period number 5.

Matching S Palace or matching N Palace

What is so important about these two palaces that matching has to take place in them?

As you know, the opposite directions of the Earlier Heaven arrangement of energies combine to a perfect balance of yin and yang, which is most auspicious.

Of all opposite directions in the Later Heaven arrangement of energies only the S and N merge to a perfect balance of yin and yang. The Palaces of the S and N have therefore singular positions in the contribution of energies in a chart.

Matching with the S or the N Palace means that either one of these two palaces is involved in the formation of Parent Trigrams.

The Parent Trigrams

The Parent Trigrams are obtained by.starting with the Period Star. One uses the sequence of the 9 periods descending by 7 or ascending by 4 to find the three numbers composing a Parent Trigram.

Sequence of the 9 periods:
1, 2, 3, 4, 5, 6, 7, 8, 9, 1, 2, 3, 4, 5, 6, 7, 8, 9, 1

- **Descending by 7**
  Starting with period 1 **descending by 7** results in number 4.
  Starting with number 4 descending by 7 results in number 7.
  The Parent Trigram is 1/4/7.

- **Ascending by 4**
  Starting with period 1 **ascending by 4** results in number 4.
  Starting with number 4 ascending by 4 results in number 7.
  The Parent Trigram is 1/4/7.

Starting with any other number of the 9 periods we will always end up in this way with the three number combinations 147, 258 and 369. These number combinations are known as the Parent Trigrams.

The Three Combination Charts (see Three Combination Charts), which can take in the strong Period Energy of all 9 periods, are made up of the three Parent Trigrams. The Seven Star Robbery Charts have only two Parent Trigrams.

Each number represents a cycle or period. Each of the three combinations contains numbers of the Upper, Middle and Lower Era as you can see below and are on account of this able to allow the strongest energy of each period to enter the chart.

Upper Era consists of the Periods **1, 2, 3**
Middle Era consists of the Periods **4, 5, 6**
Lower Era consists of the Periods **7, 8, 9**

The Three Different Interpretations of Seven Star Robbery Formations

Variation 1: Matching with the S Palace

These are charts with double Period Stars in the Facing Palace, which are matching with the S Palace as in the chart below.

Example of Matching S

Period 2 Facing S 1

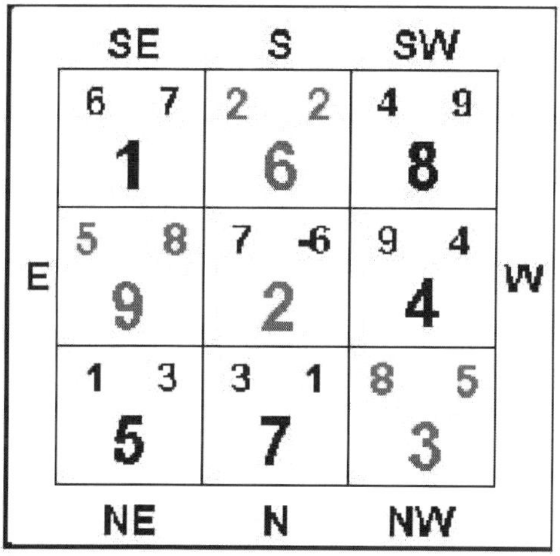

SE	S	SW
6 7 **1**	2 2 **6**	4 9 **8**
5 8 **9**	7 -6 **2**	9 4 **4**
1 3 **5**	3 1 **7**	8 5 **3**
NE	N	NW

(E left, W right)

The Facing and Mountain Stars of the S, E and NW Palaces in this chart combine to the Parent Trigram 258. The Earth Base or Time Stars in the same Palaces combine to the Parent Trigram 369.

On account of these two Parent Trigrams the strong Period Energy of the periods 2, 3, 5, 6, 8 and 9 can enter during there respective periods any building having this chart.

Variation 2: Matching with the N Palace

These are charts with double Period Stars in the Facing Palace, which are matching with the N Palace as in the chart below.

Example of Matching N

Period 2 Facing N 2/3

SE	S	SW
5 8 **1**	1 3 **6**	3 1 **8**
4 9 **9**	6 -7 **2**	8 5 **4**
9 4 **5**	2 2 **7**	7 6 **3**
NE	N	NW

(E on left side, W on right side)

The Facing and Mountain Stars of the N, W and SE Palaces in this chart combine to the Parent Trigram 258. The Earth Base or Time Stars in the same Palaces combine to the Parent Trigram 147.

On account of these two Parent Trigrams the strong Period Energy of the periods 1, 2, 4, 5, 7 and 8 can enter during there respective periods any building having this chart.

Variation 3: Double Period Star in the Facing or Sitting Palace and the Facing Star at the Facing or Sitting Palace has the number of the next period.

These are charts with double Period Stars in the Facing or Sitting Palace matching with the S or the N Palace, which have a Facing Star with the number of the next period in the Facing or Sitting Palace. The chart below has the double Period Star in the Sitting Palace and is matching with the S Palace.

Example Double Period Star in the Sitting Palace

Period 3 Facing N 2/3

SE	S	SW
8 7 **2**	3 3 **7**	1 5 **9**
9 6 **1**	-7 8 **3**	5 1 **5**
4 2 **6**	2 4 **8**	6 9 **4**
NE	N	NW

E (left side), W (right side)

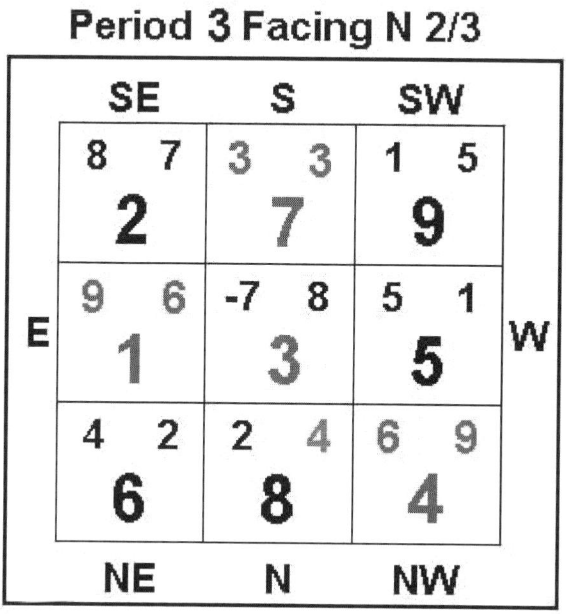

The Facing and Mountain Stars of the E, NW and S Palaces in this chart combine to the Parent Trigram 369. The Earth Base or Time Stars in the same Palaces combine to the Parent Trigram 147. The Facing Palace has a Facing Star number 4, which is the number of the next period.

On account of the two Parent Trigrams the auspicious Period Energy of the periods 1, 3, 4, 6, 7 and 9 can enter during their respective periods any building having this chart.

Example Double Period Star in the Facing Palace

Period 3 Facing N 1

	SE	S	SW	
	6　9 **2**	2　4 **7**	4　2 **9**	
E	5　1 **1**	7　-8 **3**	9　6 **5**	**W**
	1　5 **6**	3　3 **8**	8　7 **4**	
	NE	N	NW	

The double Period Star is in the Facing Palace. The Facing and Mountain Stars of the N, SE and W Palaces in this chart combine to the Parent Trigram 369. The Earth Base or Time Stars in the same Palaces combine to the Parent Trigram 258. The Sitting Palace has a Facing Star number 4, which is the number of the next period.

On account of the two Parent Trigrams the auspicious Period Energy of the periods 2, 3, 5, 6, 8 and 9 can enter during their respective periods any building having this chart.

Let us try to demystify the Variations of the Seven Star Robbery Charts

There are two questions to be asked:

1. **Which of the three variations of the Seven Star Robbery Charts is the correct one?**

2. **Do the Seven Star Robbery Formations facilitate the strong Period Star energy of all 9 periods to enter the Building?**

Is it correct that the Formation permits the strong Period Star energy of all 9 periods to enter the building?

There is a belief to this affect, which is evident in a list of charts named to have so-called Jailed Stars as in the example below.

Example of Seven Star Robbery Chart incapacitated in Period 2 by Jailed Stars

Period 3 Facing S 2/3

SE		S		SW	
7	8	3	3	5	1
2		**7**		**9**	
6	9	8	-7	1	5
1		**3**		**5**	
2	4	4	2	9	6
6		**8**		**4**	
NE		N		NW	

E / W

Period 2 Facing S 2/3

SE		S		SW	
8	5	3	1	1	3
1		**6**		**8**	
9	4	-7	6	5	8
9		**2**		**4**	
4	9	2	2	6	7
5		**7**		**3**	
NE		N		NW	

E / W

The above chart of the Seven Stars Robbery Formation of Period 3 Facing S 2/3 has in the Center Palace a Facing Star number -7. The chart of Period 2 also facing S 2/3 has in the Center Palace a Mountain Star number-7. It is therefore said that the Seven Star Robbery Chart of Period 3 Facing S 2/3 cannot take in the strong Period Star energy in Period 2 **(number 2 is not a component of the two Parent Trigrams)**. The jailed Facing and Mountain Stars number –7 are understood to prevent it.

The above is based on the assumption that a Seven Star Robbery Chart facilitates the strong Period Energy of all 9 periods to enter buildings having such a chart.

It is however not clear how this can happen, since the Seven Star Robbery Formations have only two Parent Trigrams having numbers of only 6 of the 9 periods.

Is it correct to assume that the Formation permits only the strong Period Star energy of periods having the numbers of the involved Parent Trigrams to enter the Building?

According to this opinion only the strong Period Energy of those periods, which have the numbers constituting the two Parent Trigrams, can enter the chart.

Example

Period 2 Facing N 2/3

	SE	S	SW	
	5 8 **1**	1 3 **6**	3 1 **8**	
E	4 9 **9**	6 -7 **2**	8 5 **4**	**W**
	9 4 **5**	2 2 **7**	7 6 **3**	
	NE	N	NW	

The two Parent Trigrams of the above chart are 258 and 147. Buildings having such a chart are able to take in the auspicious strong Period Star energy of those Periods, which have the numbers of their two Parent Trigrams.

This interpretation of the Seven Star Robbery Charts is the most logical one and therefore most likely the correct one.

Is it correct that the Formation permits only the strong Period Star energy of the next period to enter the building?

For this to happen it is seen to be necessary to have a Facing Star with the number of the next period in either the Facing or the Sitting Palace. Such formations are only found in the Facing Directions N 1 and N 2/3 in all periods except in period number 5.

Example

Priod 3 Facing N 2/3

SE	S	SW
8 7 **2**	3 3 **7**	1 5 **9**
E 9 6 **1**	-7 8 **3**	5 1 **5** W
4 2 **6**	2 4 **8**	6 9 **4**
NE	N	NW

Period 3 Facing N 1

SE	S	SW
6 9 **2**	2 4 **7**	4 2 **9**
E 5 1 **1**	7 -8 **3**	9 6 **5** W
1 5 **6**	3 3 **8**	8 7 **4**
NE	N	NW

Period 3 Facing N 2/3 chart having the double Period Star in the Sitting instead of the Facing Palace makes this variation of the Seven Star Robbery Chart doubtful. We know that the strength of the energies in the Facing Palace is foremost and dominant. When the energies of the Facing Palace are not involved in the formation of the two Parent Trigrams their effect is thereby reduced.

The chart Period 3 Facing N 1 is a matching N formation and therefore doesn't have the next period's number in the Parent Trigrams. The intake of the strong Period Energy of the next period wholly depends on the Facing Star in the Sitting Palace. As this Facing Star is not part of a Parent Trigram and is in the Sitting Palace its effect will be ordinary only as in the method of "Inviting the Energy of a Different Period".

This interpretation of the Seven Star Robbery Chart for the above reasons is not convincing. One may even ask what these charts have got to do with the Seven Star Robbery Formations? We could simply name them to be usable for the method "Inviting the energy of different Period".

Inviting the Energy of a Different Period

This is a well-known method applied when a new period has started, which is different from the period of the building. The Facing Star having the number of the new period has to be activated (best with a water feature) and that energy must have an open pathway to the center of the building. This method works irrespective of the palace in which the Facing Star is placed, but works best when the Facing Star is in the Facing Palace.

Is Matching S or Matching N the correct Method?

There is also confusion on this question. Both methods are correct, but matching the S is the preferred method.

It is often claimed the S has special powers to invite the strong Period Energies of future periods. This is plain nonsense, but matching the S always involves Parent Trigrams containing the number of the very next period, which is generally sought after.

A building of period 8 Facing E 1 having a Seven Star Robbery Formation matching S (Parent Trigrams 258 and 369) will enjoy the strong Period Energy of period 9 and this is what the people who have constructed the building would want.

A building of period 8 facing N 1 having a Seven Star Robbery Formation matching N (Parent Trigrams 147 and 258) will not enjoy the strong Period Energy of period 9, but the one of the next period number 1 and this is what the owners would not want to wait for.

What is meant by Robbery?

This term is misleading. When the period of the building has passed and energies are not timely and strong any more a Seven Star Robbery Formation will assure that the prosperous energy of another period can enter the building. Robbery here means: "Can make use of".

Some believe the Seven Star Robbery method can also be used during the current period of a building to rob the prosperous strong energy of the next or any other period and thereby make use of the timely energies of two periods at the same time. They also warn not to overdo the "robbing" by limiting it to 11 or 12 years only, since the "robbed" energy has to be repaid.

As one can rob only what is available and an auspicious strong Period Energy is available only in its own period, robbing the strong Period Energy of a

future period is not possible and the warning not to overdo the robbing is out of place.

What are the Benefits of the Seven Star Robbery Formations?

One is often made to believe this method is the top-secret cure-all method, which Feng Shui has to offer, but this is far from being so.

The Seven Star Robbery Formation is nothing more than a special chart, which facilitates the strong Period Energies of other than the chart's own period to enter a building in their time. The numbers of the two Parent Trigrams of the chart indicate the periods in which this is possible.

What then is the difference between the" Seven Star Robbery" method and the method of "Inviting the Energy of a different Period"?

Although both methods serve the same purpose there is a difference. The "Inviting the energy of a different Period" method requires the Facing Star of the new period to be activated and the result will depend on the strength of the activation and the placement of the star.

In case of a Seven Star Robbery chart there is no need to do anything. The strong Period Energy automatically enters the building by virtue of the Parent Trigram formations and the effect is complete.

The Ho Tu Number Combinations

The five Ho Tu number combinations represent the Five Elements. They are combinations of two energies each of the Later Heaven arrangement. They are:

Ho Tu number combinations	Compass directions	Elements
NW / N or N / NW 6 / 1 or 1 / 6	North	Water
SW / W or W / SW 2 / 7 or 7 / 2	South	Fire
NE / E or E / NE 8 / 3 or 3 / 8	East	Wood
SE / S or S / SE 4 / 9 or 9 / 4	West	Metal
Center 5 / 10 or 10 / 5	Center	Earth

Since the number 5 is in the center and number 10 is not used in Feng Shui the combinations 5 / 10 and 10 / 5 have no application in the Flying Star System.

Two Conditions

According to tradition the effects of the Ho Tu numbers will manifest themselves only under two conditions. These are:

- The Ho Tu number combinations must be in the Facing Palace
- The Ho Tu mast be made up of the Facing and the Earth Base Stars.

What is the reason for these conditions? Energies found in the Facing Palace manifest their influence in the whole building.
The Facing and the Earth Base Stars have the highest level of energy. Their interactions produce the strongest results.

The Method

When Ho Tu number combinations are present in a chart we have to consider their effect on the element of the palace in which they are located. The benevolent or malevolent effects of the Ho Tu number combinations depend on the interaction of their elements with the elements of the palaces in which they are present.

- In the interaction of the Five Elements the "full and nourishing energy coming from the front", "The direct energy coming from the same element" and "the robbing energy coming from the undefeated" are the strongest interactions of enhancement and destruction respectively. These three interactions are therefore taken as most important when considering the effect of Ho Tu number combinations.

Tradition therefore does not pay attention to the interaction of the "The small energy coming from the defeated" and "The empty energy coming from behind".

The Interactions

The combinations are benevolent when located in the direction of their own element as e.g. 1 / 6 in the north and are said to be strong there.
The combinations are benevolent also when found in the direction of the element, which their own element nourishes, as e.g. 1 / 6 in the east and southeast (water nourishes wood) and are said to be waxing there.
The combinations are malevolent when found in the direction of the element, which their own element destroys, as e.g. 1 / 6 in the south (water destroys fire) and are said to be waning there.

1 / 6 or 6 / 1 in the N, E and SE
Will greatly support intelligence and success in scholarly pursuits and research.
1 / 6 or 6 / 1 in the S
Will cause injury to head of the family. Children will be uncaring toward their parents, will become criminals and will do harm to their own family.

2 / 7 or 7 / 2 in the S, SW and NE
Will give financial success, but shady activities may be involved.
2 / 7 or 7 / 2 in the W and NW
Indicates infant death, illness and accidents.

3 / 8 or 8 / 3 in the E, SE and S
Will give loyal and supportive friends and family members.
3 / 8 or 8 / 3 in the SW and NE
Can cause suicide and severe harm to small children.

4 / 9 or 9 / 4 in the W, NW and N
Will give fabulous success in business and competitive activities.
4 / 9 or 9 / 4 in the E and SE
Bring injury or death in armed conflicts. Children will become orphans.

Ho Tu number combinations in Palaces other than the Facing Palace are not taken into account by tradition.
However, in my experience they also have their effect, but limited to the occupants and their activities in the respective palaces in which they are located.

Ho Tu number combinations of Earth Base and Mountain Star or of Facing and Mountain Star.
These Ho Tu number combinations should be considered only if a main door or any other conduit of energy such as a staircase, which by their use are suitable to activate energies, is found in the same palace.

The Ho Tu number combinations in the interaction of the Five Elements.
The formula of the Ho Tu number combinations is based on only three of the five interactions of the elements. These are:

1. The full and nourishing energy coming from the front (waxing and benevolent).
2. The direct energy coming from the same element itself (strong and benevolent).
3. The robbing energy coming from the undefeated (waning and malevolent).

In my opinion it is worthwhile to consider also the other two interactions of the elements. These are:

1. The small energy coming from the defeated (waxing and benevolent).
2. The empty energy coming from behind (waning and malevolent).

How to Cure the Waning Position of Ho Tu Number

Combinations

Cure the waning position of the Ho Tu number combinations

2/7 or 7/2 with water
1/6 or 6/1 with wood
3/8 or 8/3 with fire
4/9 or 9/4 with water

The Additive Effect

This is a technique based on the positive (yang) or negative (yin) character of the stars (see The Energies of the Eight Directions) and the different levels of strength of the Earth Base, the Facing and the Mountain Star to identify the energy, which is dominant in a palace. If the dominant energy is yang (stars number 1, 4, 6 and 8) it can neutralize the yin energy (stars number 2, 3, 5, 7 and 9).

- A benevolent Facing Star can neutralize a malevolent Earth Base.
- A benevolent Earth Base can neutralize a malevolent Mountain Star
- The combined energy of a benevolent Earth Base and a benevolent Mountain Star can neutralize a malevolent Facing Star
- When the benevolent star or stars get engaged in the process of neutralizing a malevolent star, they will get used up and will lose their own energy.

When applying the method of Additive Effects the interaction of the Five Elements is not taken into account.

Stars with the numbers 3 and 7 when applying the Additive Effect are considered to have a neutral character, since they do not take part in neutralizing other stars, nor do other stars neutralize them.

The Interaction of Benevolent Stars

When all three stars in a palace are benevolent their interaction with each other is often ignored. Except for the combination of Earth Base number 8 and Facing Star number 4 the interaction of benevolent stars was seen to constitute an adding up of positive energies not interfering with each other.

This practice has been carried over to us from a time when living conditions were far more flexible than today. Areas with malevolent energies were avoided and those with benevolent energies were made use of. It is also from this earlier time that the use of the colour red as a general enhancer has come to us and is still in practice.

Applying countermeasures and enhancers, as we do today, in order to harmonize living space was generally not seen as necessary then and was brought into use at later times, when conditions of living became more and more restricted.

In keeping our objectives in mind, when dealing with the interaction of benevolent stars, we must be careful not to weaken their energies. We may therefore not use the "empty energy coming from behind" and the "robbing energy coming from the undefeated".

To establish harmony is a high ideal, but sometimes we may want to do without it, hoping for certain effects which we desire. A strong benevolent star is therefore often our aim, even at the expense of harmony.

The Method

Step 1. Look at the palace and see what stars are there. If all three stars are of the benevolent group (1, 4, 6, 8), identify the Earth Base, the Facing and the Mountain Star.

Star combination 6/1/4

Step 2. If Earth Base is number 1, the Facing Star is number 4 and the Mountain Star is number 6, we have to find out, how the Facing and the Mountain Star interact with the Earth Base Star.

Step 3. Facing Star 4 is the empty energy coming from behind, which drains the energy of the Earth Base 1, but the Mountain Star 6, which is the full and nourishing energy coming from the front, enhances the Earth Base. From this we can understand that the energies in this palace are in harmony with each other and nothing needs to be done. The same will apply if the Facing Star is number 6 and the Mountain Star is number 4.

Star combination 8/1/4

Step 2. If Earth Base is number 1, the Facing Star is number 4 and the Mountain Star is number 8,

Step 3. The Facing Star 4 is the empty energy coming from behind, which drains the energy of the Earth Base 1. In addition to this the Mountain Star 8 represents the robbing energy coming from the undefeated, which destroys the energy of the Earth Base 1.

Step 4. To balance the effect, which the Mountain Star has on the Earth Base, we have to use fire element as countermeasure which is the small energy coming from the defeated. Using fire element as countermeasure will also reduce the draining effect, which the 4 has on the 1, but to harmonize the energies metal should also be applied to cope as the nourishing energy coming from the front with the draining energy of the 4 coming from behind. The same will apply if the Facing Star is number 8 and the Mountain Star is number 4.

Star combination 6/1/8

Step 2. The Earth Base is number 1. The Facing Star is number 8 and the Mountain Star is number 6.

Step 3. The Facing Star 8 is the robbing energy coming from the undefeated. The mountain Star 6 is the full and nourishing energy coming from the front, enhancing the Earth Base, which is desirable.

Step 4. The effect the Facing Star has on the Earth Base 1 has to be balanced by applying fire element representing the small energy coming from the defeated. In order to establish harmony wood may be used as countermeasure to balance the effect the metal element of the 6 has on the water element of the 1. However, it is desirable to nourish the water element of the 1 and should therefore better not be done. The same will apply, if the Facing Star is number 6 and the Mountain Star is number 8.

Star combination 6/4/1

Step 2. The Earth Base is number 4, the Facing Star is number 1 and the Mountain Star is number 6,

Step 3. The Facing Star 1 is the full and nourishing energy coming from the front, which will enhance the energy of the Earth Base 4. The Mountain Star 6 is the robbing energy coming from the undefeated, which destroys the energy of the Earth Base.

Step 4. To balance the effect the Mountain Star 6 has on the Earth Base 4 , we have to use earth element as countermeasure which is the small energy coming from the defeated. In order to establish harmony fire may be used as a countermeasure to balance the effect the water element of the 1 has on the wood element of the 4. In this way we will establish harmony. However, since it is desirable to nourish the wood element of the 4, it had therefore better not be done. The same will apply, if the Facing Star is number 6 and the Mountain Star is number 1.

Star combination 6/4/8

Step 2. The Earth Base is number 4, the Facing Star is number 8 and the Mountain Star is number 6.

Step 3. The Facing Star 8 is the small energy coming from the defeated and the Mountain Star is the robbing energy coming from the undefeated. This combination shows energies in harmony and nothing needs to be done. However, it will be advisable to use a water feature to nourish the wood element of Earth Base 4 without disturbing the harmony. The same will apply if the Facing Star is number 6 and the Mountain Star is number 8.

Star combination 1/4/8

Step 2. The Earth Base is number 4, the Facing Star is number 8 and the Mountain Star is number 1.

Step 3. The Facing Star 8 is the small energy coming from the defeated and the Mountain Star 1 is the full and nourishing energy coming from the front, which is desirable.

Step 4. To balance the effect the Facing Star has on the Earth Base we could apply the metal element, which is the robbing energy coming from the undefeated and for the effect of the water element of the 1 we could use the fire element as countermeasure which is the empty energy coming from behind. In this way we will establish harmony.

Step 5. Keeping our objectives in mind we may however not use the metal element as countermeasure, since it would weaken both the benevolent stars 4 and 8 and may not use the fire element either, which would drain the energy of the Earth Base 4.

Considering this, it may be better not to apply any countermeasures at all. The same will apply if the Facing Star is number 1 and the Mountain Star is number 8.

Star combination 1/6/4

Step 2. The Earth Base is number 6, the Facing Star is number 4 and the Mountain Star is number 1.

Step 3. The Facing Star 4 is the small energy coming from the defeated and the Mountain Star 1 is the empty energy coming from behind.

Step 4. To balance the effect the Facing Star has on the Earth Base, we should apply the fire element, which is the robbing energy coming from the undefeated and to balance the effect of the Mountain Star we should use the earth element, which is the full and nourishing energy coming from the front. In this way we will establish harmony.

Step 5. Keeping our objectives in mind we may not use the fire element, since it would weaken the benevolent Facing Star 4 and destroy the energy of the Earth Base 6. The same will apply if the Facing Star is number 1 and the Mountain Star is number 4.

Star combination 1/6/8

Step 2. The Earth Base is number 6, the Facing Star is number 8 and the Mountain Star is number 1

Step 3. The Facing Star 8 is the full and nourishing energy coming from the front, which will enhance the energy of the Earth Base 6. The Mountain Star 1 is the empty energy coming from behind. This combination shows energies in harmony and nothing needs to be done. The same will apply if the Facing Star is number 1 and the Mountain Star is number 8.

Star combination 4/6/8

Step 2. The Earth Base is number 6, the Facing Star is number 8 and the Mountain Star is number 4.

Step 3. The Facing Star 8 is the full and nourishing energy coming from the front, which will enhance the energy of the Earth Base 6. The Mountain Star 4 is the small energy coming from the defeated.

Step 4. To balance the effect the small energy coming from the defeated has on the Earth Base we should use the fire element. To balance the effect the Facing Star 8 has on the Earth Base 6, we should apply water as countermeasure. In this way we will establish harmony.

Step 5. In keeping our objectives in mind we should not use the fire element, since it would weaken the benevolent Mountain Star and destroy the energy of the Earth Base and a water feature will also weaken the energy of the Earth Base. Therefore nothing needs to be done.

The same will apply if the Facing Star is number 4 and the Mountain Star is number 8.

Star combination 1/8/4

Step 2. The Earth Base is number 8, the Facing Star is number 4 and the Mountain Star is number 1.

Step 3. The Facing Star 4 is the robbing energy coming from the undefeated and the Mountain Star 1 is the small energy coming from the defeated. This combination shows energies in harmony and nothing needs to be done. The same will apply if the Facing Star is number 1 and the Mountain Star is number 4.

Step 4. However, when applying the fire element we can even improve the energy of the Earth Base without harming the Facing Star 4, since this star is nourished by the Mountain Star 1. The same will apply if the Facing Star is number 1 and the Mountain Star is number 4.

Star combination 1/8/6

Step 2. The Earth Base is number 8, the Facing Star is number 6 and the Mountain Star is number 1.

Step 3. The Facing Star 6 is the empty energy coming from behind and the Mountain Star 1 is the small energy coming from the defeated.

Step 4. To balance the effect the Facing Star has on the Earth Base we have to use the fire element. The effect the Mountain Star has on the Earth Base could be balanced by using the wood element as a countermeasure. In this way we will establish harmony.

Step 5. Keeping our objectives in mind we should not use the wood element as countermeasure since it would weaken the energy of the Mountain Star and destroy the energy of the Earth Base. The same will apply if the Facing Star is number 1 and the Mountain Star is number 6.

Star combination 4/8/6

Step 2. The Earth Base is number 8, the Facing Star is number 6 and the Mountain Star is number 4.

Step 3. The Facing Star 6 is the empty energy coming from behind and the Mountain Star 4 is the robbing energy coming from the undefeated.

Step 4. To balance the effect the Facing Star has on the Earth Base, we have to use the fire element. The effect the Mountain Star has on the Earth Base can be balanced with water, which is the small energy coming from the undefeated. In this way we will establish harmony.

The same applies when number 4 is the Facing Star and number 6 is the Mountain Star.

How to Deal with Malevolent Stars

deal with malevolent stars is the foremost task in any Feng Shui practice. The energies of stars number 2 and 5 cause disease, loss of wealth, obstacles in any undertakings, misfortune of any kind and even death. Protection from these energies is therefore understood to be the primary concern.

The star number 9 on account of its ability to enhance the stars number 2 and 5 and defeat the stars number 6 and 7 is also a major target in all Flying Star Feng Shui efforts.

The numbers 3 and 7 are not seen as being malevolent by themselves, but are understood to be so in certain combinations with other stars.

Star number 5

The energy of star number 5 has no trigram in both, the Earlier and the Later Heaven and we therefore don't know its yin / yang composition. Number 5 doesn't combine with any of the other energies to a perfect balance of yin and yang. It is always most malevolent and mysterious. The ideal counter measure for a star number 5 is the metal element of number 6.

In combination with number 8 the effect of number 5 depends on the level of energy of both stars. Since both stars represent the same element they reinforce each other. If number 8 is the Facing Star, which carries the highest level of energy, its benevolent energy will conquer the malevolent energy of an Earth Base or Mountain Star number 5 and this combination is not harmful. It is however better to be on the safe side and use the metal element of number 6 as countermeasure.

The combination 4/5 is bad and should be treated with the metal element of number 6. The same holds true for the combination 1/5.

For special combinations with star number 5 see under star numbers 2, 3, 7, and 9.

Star number 2

The energy of star number 2 is all yin, which stands for contraction and decay. The perfect countermeasure is the metal element of number 6, which drains number 2 of its energy, and more than that the energies of both numbers combine to a perfect balance of yin and yang, which is auspicious.

In combination with number 7 it represents the fire element and is auspicious in the S, SW and NE palaces, but inauspicious in the E and SE palaces.

In combination with number 8 the effect of number 2 depends on the level of energy of both stars. Since both stars represent the same element they reinforce each other. If number 8 is the Facing Star, which carries the highest level of energy, its benevolent energy will conquer the malevolent energy of an Earth Mountain Star number 2 and this combination is not harmful.

In case number 2 is the Facing Star and number 8 is the Earth Base or Mc __. Star the malevolent energy of number 2 conquers the benevolent energy of number 8 and gets reinforced by it. This is a dangerous combination and has to be cured. The metal element of number 6 is the best countermeasure. Number 6 creates perfect harmony of yin and yang when it combines with number 2 without harming the benevolent energy of number 8, since the combination 6 / 8 on account of the fact that both energies are benevolent is one of the most auspicious combinations known in Feng Shui.

In combination with number 9 the malevolent strength of number 2 gets enhanced, becomes more dangerous and needs to be cured. The metal element of number 6 alone is not enough and has to be supplemented with water, since number 9 continues enhancing number 2.

The combination with number 5 is equally dangerous and needs the metal element of number 6 as countermeasure.

Tradition says the combination with number 3 needs the fire element as countermeasure. However, if number 3 is the Facing and number 2 the Earth Base or Mountain Star the water element is needed as countermeasure. When number 2 is the Facing and number 3 the Earth Base or Mountain Star the metal element of number 6 is the best countermeasure.

When number 2 is the host energy the combination with number 1 needs the metal element of number 6 as countermeasure.

The combination with number 4 needs the metal element of number 6 as countermeasure when number 2 is the Facing and number 4 the Earth Base or Mountain Star. If number 4 is the Facing and number 2 the Earth Base or Mountain Star, water and metal element features are needed as countermeasure.

Star number 9

Will be very benevolent when in combination with number 8 and especially so if number 9 is the Facing and number 8 the Earth Base Star. The combination with number 6 or 7 is malevolent, especially when number 9 is the guest energy. The earth element of number 8 is needed then as countermeasure.

In case of the combination of 9 / 7 / 5 the best solution for this problem is water and the metal of number 7.

The combination 9/1 creates perfect harmony of yin and yang and is auspicious.

The combination 9/4 represents the metal element and is auspicious in the W, NW and N but malevolent in the E and SE where water should be used as countermeasure.

For the combination 9/3 also use water as countermeasure.

For the very malevolent combination 9/5 use water and metal countermeasures.

Star number 7

The combination of number 7 with star number 6 is very malicious and must be cured. Water is the recommended traditional cure, but the earth element of number 8 will also work very well, if not better, since the combinations 8/6 and 8/7 are both very benevolent.

The combinations 7/3 and 3/7 are both causing trouble and distress. Water is the remedy. The same applies to 7/4 and 4/7 although these two combinations are not known to have a malevolent effect and could be left as they are.

The combinations 5/7 and 7/5 are malefic and should be treated. To break up the combination water is ideal, but it will enhance number 5, which should be avoided if possible. I suggest using the earth element of number 8 to do the needful.

The combination 7/8 is perfect harmony of yin and yang and is very benevolent.

The combination 7/1 is said to be beneficial and need not be treated.

Star number 3.

Star number 3 combined with number 2 is one of the well known very malefic combinations causing greatest disharmony amongst people. The traditional cure is the fire element, which breaks up the combination, but enhances number 2 which will be a lesser evil than the combination in itself. I suggest trying water and metal as countermeasure. The combination 3/4 is perfect harmony of yin and yang and is very benevolent.

The combination 3/8 represents the wood element and is very auspicious in the E, SE and S but malevolent elsewhere and especially so in the SW and NE where the fire element can be used to cure the harmful affect.

The combination 3/1 has a special affect when found in the W and produces many descendents. Elsewhere in the chart this combination is negative and needs a metal countermeasure of number 6. The fire element as countermeasure will also very well work.

The combination 3/5 is a combination of negative energies and also needs the metal element of number 6 as a countermeasure. The combination 3/9 is bad and should be cured with water.

Countermeasures and Enhancers

Countermeasures are used in accordance with the system of the Five Elements, to weaken malevolent energy and enhance benevolent energy.

Metal Element

Metal as Countermeasure

Metal is the most often used countermeasure. Traditionally it is used for the malevolent numbers 2 and 5. Metal drains the energy of both numbers, which belong to the earth element.

When applying the metal element as countermeasure, we have the choice of metal as represented by number 6 or by number 7. Number 6 is metal proper such as gold, brass or any other metal. Moving metal like a metal pendulum of a clock is more effective and so is the sound of metal, as sound is in itself another manifestation of the metal element.

Metal of number 6 as countermeasure will combine with number 2 creating perfect harmony of yin and yang. This combination is very auspicious.

If you have the combination of 2/8 or 8/2 you can still use metal as a countermeasure for the malevolent 2 of the combination without harming the benevolent number 8, since the combination 6/8 is one of the best energy combinations known in Flying Star Feng Shui.

As you will have understood from the above, metal is the ideal countermeasure for the malevolent earth element stars 2 and 5 while it does no harm to the number 8. Keeping this in mind the use of metal bells, gongs and wind chimes in ceremonies to purify places of negative energies, which you may have thought of as being nothing more than meaningless rituals, will now make sense.

The so-called saltwater cure is a countermeasure representing the metal element of number 7. This countermeasure consists of a glass bowl filled with table salt and topped up with just enough water to cover the salt. Many practitioners place some metal coins on the salt and argue on the number of coins to be used. They use silver coins and other metal coins in combinations of 4/9 and 1/6 hoping to achieve special affects.

In my view this is purely symbolic and should not be done since the number 7 metal element of the saltwater and the number 6 metal element of the coins make the combination 7/6, which is very malevolent.

The saltwater countermeasure will combine with number 2 to create the combinations 2/7 or 7/2, which are the Ho Tu number combinations for the Fire

Element. These combinations are auspicious in some and inauspicious in other directions (see Ho Tu Number Combinations).

If the saltwater countermeasure were used for a 2/8 star combination the combinations 2/7 and 8/7 would be produced. While the combination 2/7 is the Fire Element, the combination 8/7 is perfect harmony of yin and yang and is very auspicious.

If you have difficulties to understand how saltwater can be effective as a metal element countermeasure, please remember that the metal element is an energy, which directs its force from all directions towards one central point. When you think of the hydroscopic action of salt, which attracts to itself water from all directions, you will understand the metal element nature of this cure.

Metal as Enhancer

Metal is used to enhance the Water Element. Using metal number 6 will create the combination 6/1, which is very auspicious for money matters. The 6/1 is also a Ho Tu number combination, which represents the water element and creates auspicious effects in the N, E and SE palaces, but is malevolent in the S palace.

Don't use countermeasures representing the energy of number 6 when a star number 7 is present in the same palace. The metal element of number 7 should be used in such a case instead.

Earth Element

Earth as Countermeasure

The earth element is represented by the numbers 2, 5 and 8. Number 8 earth element is found in small stones and is used as countermeasure for the malevolent star combination 6/9 when number 6 is the host energy. Applying earth element of number 8 will result in the combinations 9/8 and 6/8 which are both very benevolent.

In case of the malevolent combination 7/9 when number 7 is the host energy the same countermeasure will produce the combinations 9/8 and 7/8 which are also very benevolent.

Earth as Enhancer

Earth is used to enhance the star number 6. This will generate the combination 8/6 which is a very auspicious combination.

The earth element of number 8 as countermeasure and enhancer can be a glass bowl or container filled with small rounded stones. Don't take stones with sharp edges.

Fire Element

Fire as Countermeasure
Fire is used as countermeasure to reduce the energy of the stars number 3 and 4. in the combinations 3/2 and 2/3 as well as for the combination 8/4 and 8/3 in which the wood element hurts the earth element of number 8.

Fire as Enhancer
Fire is a very valuable enhancer for star number 8 and will produce the combination 8/9 which will give excellent happy relationships with family and friends.

Red articles, strong light and fire as such will serve very well as enhancer or countermeasure.
Never use the fire element when number 2 and / or number 5 are present.

Wood Element

Wood as Countermeasure
The wood Element is never used as countermeasure in Feng Shui, but can be used to balance the energies of the stars in a palace to create harmony (see under Five Elements).

Wood as Enhancer
The wood Element is never used as enhancer in Feng Shui, but can be used to balance the energies of the stars in a palace to create harmony (see under Five Elements).

The wood element of number 3 is best represented by fast growing plants such as green bamboo, reed and cane.
The wood element of number 4 is found in tall wooden objects.

Water Element

Water as Countermeasure
Water is used as countermeasure for the fire star number 9. Water in Feng Shui is understood not only to dowse fire, but the energies of water and fire combine to create perfect harmony of yin and yang. The ideal countermeasure to combat the ill effects of fire is therefore water.
Water is also used for the malefic star combination 3/7 and 7/3.

Water as Enhancer

Water is used to enhance the energy of star number 4 and can be used to balance the energies of the stars in a palace to create harmony (see under Five Elements).

Water, which moves, has a stronger effect. Waterfalls, fountains and even a glass bowl filled with water can be used.

Never use water when numbers 2 and/or 5 are present. You will however have to use water when there is also number 9.

To this group belong:

Facing Star Formula
Period Star Formula
Castle Gate Formula

Formulas without Time Factor

These formulae are not based on any time factor, but on harmony features of energies. They are believed to be more effective than the time related formulas. To this group belong:

The Eight Dragon Gate Water Formulas
The Five Ghosts Carry Money Formula
The Formula of perfect Directional Harmony

Facing Star Water Formula

Based on Time Factor and Directional Exposure

Some schools use water features to activate the timely Facing Stars to enhance prosperity and wealth prospects. When doing so they often pay no attention to the interaction water will have on the elements of the stars in the area. Their main consideration is the timeliness of the energy of the prosperous and growing Facing Stars (see Level of strength of the Facing Stars according to their timeliness).

Level of Strength of the Facing Stars according to their Timeliness

Energy of stars	The 9 Periods								
	1	2	3	4	5	6	7	8	9
Prosperous	1	2	3	4	5	6	7	8	9
Growing	2 3	3 4	4 5	5 6	6 7	7 8	8 9	9 1	1 2
Retreating	9	1	2	3	4	5	6	7	8
Dead	6 7	9 6	1 6	2 8	2 3	4 9	5 4 3	2 6	6 7
Killing	5	5 7	7 9	7 9	2 9	2 3	2 3	3 4 5	3 4 5

Example

During the period of 7 the Facing Star number **7 is prosperous** and the Facing Stars number **8 and 9 are growing.**
Water features at the location of Facing Stars 7, 8 and 9 and water flowing from the respective directions, is said to activate these stars to enhancing wealth prospects.

Period 7 Building Facing E2

1　6	5　1	3　8
6	**2**	**4**
2　7	9　5	7　3
5	**7**	**9**
6　2	4　9	4
1	**3**	**8**

(←)

For Facing Star number 7 water should be placed in the E and should flow from the E.
For Facing Star number 8 water should be placed in the SW and should flow from the SW
For Facing Star number 9 water should be placed in the N and should flow from the N.

Can we ignore the Interaction of the Five Elements?

Failure has been experienced in period 7 to activate the timely Facing Star number 7 with water features. Some schools have called this an exception to the rule. They are the schools, which use water features to activate Facing Stars irrespective of the interaction water will have with the element of the Facing Stars.

I think from the above we could safely conclude that on account of the activity of flowing water and, keeping in mind that water is a strong carrier of energy and the Facing Stars represent the direction from which energy enters a building, water features will activate Facing Stars. The water will however also affect the energy of the stars in the interaction of the Five Elements.
Since water will drain the energy of the metal element, it will deplete a Facing Star number 7.

Water Features plus Counter Measures for Facing Stars

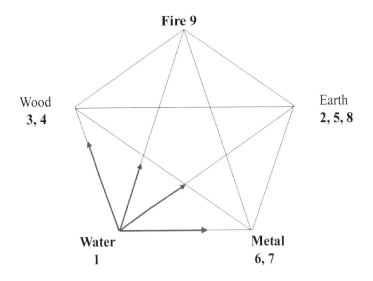

A Facing Star 1, 3 and 4

will benefit doubly from a water feature. These stars, especially No. 3 and 4 will benefit from the activity of flowing water as well as from the effect water has on them in the interaction of the five elements.

A Facing Star 6 and 7

will benefit from the activity of flowing water, but will suffer from the interaction of water with their metal element. They will get drained of their energies.

A Facing Star 9

will get defeated by water. However, when water and the fire element of number 9 come together, they form a union of perfect harmony of yin and yang. This is one of the harmony features of the Earlier Heaven arrangement of energies and is most auspicious.

A Facing Star 2, 5 and 8

Contrary to the opinion that water will weaken these stars, they are actually enhanced by it. Water features are Guest energies, which act on the Host Energy of the Facing Stars.

When the earth element (2, 5, 8) acts on water, it will destroy water. When water acts on the earth element, it will enhance the earth (see interaction of the Five Elements).

Water Formula of Heavenly Harmony

This formula is disclosed and published here for the very first time.

The Formula is based on the Earlier Heaven Harmony Feature of perfectly balanced yin and yang, which is applied to the Facing Stars in the Facing and Sitting Palace.
The beneficial effect of the formula is strongest when one of the Facing Stars has the period number and the other has the number of the next period such as 7 and 8, 9 and 1 and 3 and 4.

The Formula uses the Facing Stars of the Facing and the Sitting Palace. When the combination of both Facing Stars present perfect harmony of yin and yang and Water flows from both directions, wealth prospects are greatly enhanced.

The Earlier Heaven Harmony Feature

The opposing directions of the Earlier Heaven arrangement of energies when combined make three yang and three yin lines. This is perfect harmony of yin and yang energies and is most fortunate.

Earlier Heaven
Arrangement of Energies

Later Heaven
Arrangement of Energies

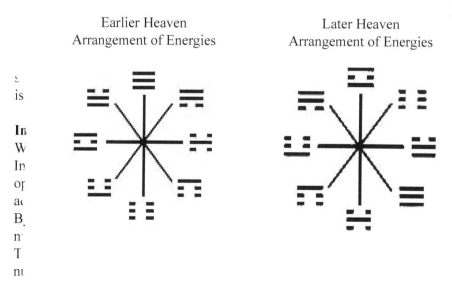

Earlier Heaven Harmony Feature in Later Heaven

Perfect harmony of yin and yang in the Later Heaven arrangement is found in the combinations of :

SW combined with NW
W combined with NE
E combined with SE
S combined with N

Perfect Heavenly Harmony occurs only in Buildings of:

Period 1 Facing Direction S1, S2, S3
Period 2 Facing Direction W1, W2, W3
Period 3 Facing Direction N1, N2, N3
Period 4 Facing Direction S1, S2, S3
Period 6 Facing Direction E1, E2, E3
Period 7 Facing Direction N1, N2, N3
Period 8 Facing Direction S1, S2, S3
Period 9 Facing Direction N1, N2, N3

Example

Period 7   Period 7

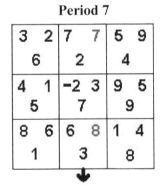

Facing N2/3   Facing N1

The Directions from which Water should flow

Building of period 7 facing N1
should have water flowing from the direction of N1 and S1.

Building of period 7 facing N2
should have water flowing from the direction of N2 and S2.

Building of period 7 facing N3
should have water flowing from the direction of N3 and S3.

The same Formula can also be applied on Facing Stars of other Palaces

Energy, which enters a building from the Facing Direction, is strongest and spreads throughout the building. To have benevolent energies in the Facing Palace is therefore considered very fortunate in Flying Star Feng Shui.

The "Water Formula of Heavenly Harmony" uses the energies of the Facing Stars in the Facing and the Sitting Palaces as these are the strongest energies which will give the strongest effect when combined in perfect harmony of yin and yang.

However, the same can be attempted by using the energies of Facing Stars located in other palaces. The effect produced that way will be much reduced when compared with the effect obtained by combining the energies of the Facing Stars in the Facing and Sitting Palaces.

Following the same principle we use the energy of Facing Stars, which combine in perfect harmony of yin and yang.

Example
Building of Period 7 Facing S1

2 3 6	7 7 2	9 5 4
1 4 5	3 -2 7	5 9 9
6 8 1	8 6 3	4 1 8

The Directions from which Water should flow

Facing Stars 3 and 4 combine in perfect harmony of YIN and YANG. Water should flow from the directions of SE1 and E1. The water features should preferably be set up in the SE and/or the E palace.

Facing Stars 7 and 8 combine in perfect harmony of YIN and YANG. Water should flow from the directions of S1 and NE1. The water features should preferably be set up in the S and/or the NE palace.

Facing Stars 9 and 1 combine in perfect harmony of YIN and YANG. Water should flow from the directions of W1 and NW1. The water features should preferably be set up in the NW and/or the W palace.

Warning

It is not advisable to use for a building more that one combination of Facing Stars, which combine in perfect harmony of YIN and YANG. Using two or more combinations will cause a turbulence of energies, which can bring very harmful effects

The Eight Dragon Gate Water Formulas

These are:
1. **The Earlier Heaven Water Method**
2. **The Later Heaven Water Method**
3. **The Heavenly Robber Water Position**
4. **The Earth Punishment Water Position**
5. **The Courtyard Robber Water Position**
6. **The Visitor Water Position**
7. **The Guest Water Position**
8. **The Auxiliary Water Position**

Sitting Directions	N	SW	E	SE	NW	W	NE	S
Earlier Heaven	W	N	NE	SW	S	SE	NW	E
Later Heaven	SW	SE	S	W	NE	N	E	NW
Heavenly Robber	SE	W	NW	N	E	SW	S	NE
Earth Punishment	SW	N	NE	W	S	SE	E	NW
Courtyard Robber	S	NE	W	NW	SE	E	SW	N
Visitor	E	NW	SE	S	SW	NE	N	W
Guest	NW	E	N	NE	W	S	SE	SW
Auxiliary Trigram	NE	S	SW	E	N	NW	W	SE

Each of the Dragon Gate Water Formulas

Is based on the interaction of the Two Heavens and some of them also on the Harmony Features of the Two Heavens

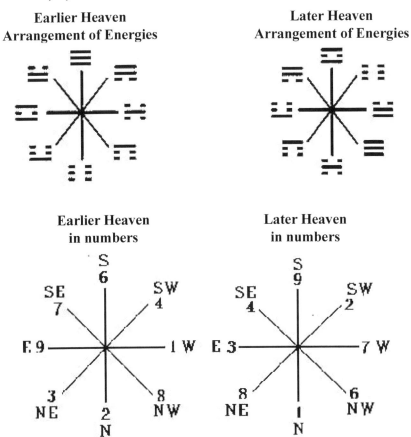

**Earlier Heaven
Arrangement of Energies**

**Later Heaven
Arrangement of Energies**

**Earlier Heaven
in numbers**

**Later Heaven
in numbers**

The Harmony Features

In the Earlier Heaven arrangement of energies the opposing compass directions when combined make perfect harmony of yin and yang

In the Later Heaven arrangement of energies the opposing compass directions when combined always make the sum of 10.

Water Formula of the Earlier Heaven

This Formula is based on the Sitting Direction and the Interaction of the Earlier and Later Heaven. No Time Factor involved.

This is a famous and easy to apply Water Formula. The flow of water from a direction indicated in the Earlier Heaven is said to be very powerful to enhance prospects for loyal and supportive relationships and good health.
Water flowing away in that direction causes illness and early death.

Later Heaven Sitting Directions

Sitting Directions	1	2	3	4	6	7	8	9
Earlier Heaven Directions	7	1	8	2	9	4	6	3

Sitting Directions	N	SW	E	SE	NW	W	NE	S
Earlier Heaven Directions	W	N	NE	SW	S	SE	NW	E

Good

When water comes from the Earlier Heaven direction it is good for health and loyal supportive relationships.

Bad

When water exits in the Earlier Heaven direction it is bad for health and relationships.

Examples

Building is sitting in the North
The N in the Later Heaven has the number 1, which in the Earlier Heaven is in the W. Water flowing from the W is therefore good for relationships, harmony with people and good for health.

Building is sitting in the Southwest

The SW in the Later Heaven has the number 2, which in the Earlier Heaven is in the N. Water flowing from the N is therefore good for relationships, harmony with people and good for health.

Building is sitting in the East

The E in the Later Heaven has the number 3, which in the Earlier Heaven is in the NE. Water flowing from the NE is therefore good for relationships, harmony with people and good for health.

Building is sitting in the Southeast

The SE in the Later Heaven has the number 4, which in the Earlier Heaven is in the SW. Water flowing from the SW is therefore good for relationships, harmony with people and good for health.

Building is sitting in the Northwest

The NW in the Later Heaven has the number 6, which in the Earlier Heaven is in the S. Water flowing from the S is therefore good for relationships, harmony with people and good for health

Building is sitting in the West

The W in the Later Heaven has the number 7, which in the Earlier Heaven is in the SE. Water flowing from the SE is therefore good for relationships, harmony with people and good for health.

Building is sitting in the Northeast

The NE in the Later Heaven has the number 8, which in the Earlier Heaven is in the NW. Water flowing from the NW is therefore good for relationships, harmony with people and good for health.

Building is sitting in the South

The S in the Later Heaven has the number 9, which in the Earlier Heaven is in the E. Water flowing from the E is therefore good for relationships, harmony with people and good for health.

Water Formula of the Later Heaven

This Formula is based on the Sitting Direction and the Interaction of the Earlier and Later Heaven. No Time Factor involved.

This is a famous and easy to apply Water Formula. The flow of water from a direction indicated in the Later Heaven is said to be very powerful to enhance wealth

Later Heaven Sitting Directions

Sitting Directions	1	2	3	4	6	7	8	9
Later Heaven Directions	2	4	9	7	8	1	3	6

Sitting Directions	N	SW	E	SE	NW	W	NE	S
Later Heaven Directions	SW	SE	S	W	NE	N	E	NW

Good

When water comes from the Later Heaven direction it is good for Wealth.

Bad

When water exits in the Later Heaven direction loss of fortunes is indicated.

Examples

Building is sitting in the North
The N in the Earlier Heaven has number 2, which in the Later Heaven is in the SW. Water flowing from the SW is therefore good for wealth.

Building is sitting in the Southwest
The SW in the Earlier Heaven has number 4, which in the Later Heaven is in the SE. Water flowing from the SE is therefore good for wealth.

Building is sitting in the East

The E in the Earlier Heaven has number 9, which in the Later Heaven is in the S. Water flowing from the S is therefore good for wealth.

Building is sitting in the Southeast

The SE in the Earlier Heaven has number 7, which in the Later Heaven is in the W. Water flowing from the W is therefore good for wealth.

Building is sitting in the Northwest

The NW in the Earlier Heaven has number 8, which in the Later Heaven is in the NE. Water flowing from the northeast is therefore good for wealth.

Building is sitting in the West

The W in the Earlier Heaven has number 1, which in the Later Heaven is in the N. Water flowing from the N is therefore good for wealth.

Building is sitting in the Northeast

The NE in the Earlier Heaven has number 3, which in the Later Heaven is in the E. Water flowing from the E is therefore good for wealth.

Building is sitting in the South

The S in the Earlier Heaven has number 6, which in the Later Heaven is in the NW. Water flowing from the northwest is therefore good for wealth.

Heavenly Robber Water Position

This formula is based on the position of trigrams in the Earlier and in the Later Heaven. No Time Factor involved.

When water comes from the Heavenly Robber direction it is said to cause long-lasting illnesses.

When Water flows out in that direction prosperity is indicated.

Later Heaven Sitting Directions

Sitting Direction	N	SW	E	SE	NW	W	NE	S
Heavenly Robber	SE	W	NW	N	E	SW	S	NE

Sitting Direction	1	2	3	4	6	7	8	9
Heavenly Robber	4	7	6	1	3	2	9	8

Examples

Building has Sitting Direction N

In the Later Heaven the N has a trigram or number, which in the Earlier Heaven is in the W. The trigram of the W in the Later Heaven is in the SE of the Earlier Heaven, which is the Heavenly Robber direction.

Building has Sitting Direction SW

In the Later Heaven the SW has a trigram or number, which in the Earlier Heaven is in the N. The trigram of the N in the Later Heaven is in the W of the Earlier Heaven, which is the Heavenly Robber direction.

Building has Sitting Direction E

In the Later Heaven the E has a trigram or number, which in the Earlier Heaven is in the NE. The trigram of the NE in the Later Heaven is in the NW of the Earlier Heaven, which is the Heavenly Robber direction.

Building has Sitting Direction SE

In the Later Heaven the SE has a trigram or number, which in the Earlier Heaven is in the SW. The trigram of the SW in the Later Heaven is in the N of the Earlier Heaven, which is the Heavenly Robber direction.

Building has Sitting Direction NW

In the Later Heaven the NW has a trigram or number, which in the Earlier Heaven is in the S. The trigram of the S in the Later Heaven is in the E of the Earlier Heaven, which is the Heavenly Robber direction.

Building has Sitting Direction W

In the Later Heaven the W has a trigram or number, which in the Earlier Heaven is in the SE. The trigram of the SE in the Later Heaven is in the SW of the Earlier Heaven, which is the Heavenly Robber direction.

Building has Sitting Direction NE

In the Later Heaven the NE has a trigram or number, which in the Earlier Heaven is in the NW. The trigram of the NW in the Later Heaven is in the S of the Earlier Heaven, which is the Heavenly Robber direction.

Building has Sitting Direction S

In the Later Heaven the S has a trigram or number, which in the Earlier Heaven is in the E. The trigram of the E in the Later Heaven is in the NE of the Earlier Heaven, which is the Heavenly Robber direction.

Earth Punishment Water Position

This formula is based on the position of trigrams in the Earlier and in the Later Heaven. No Time Factor involved.

Having a door there or water coming from or going to the Earth Punishment direction is said to be inauspicious for women.

Later Heaven Sitting Directions

Sitting Direction	N	SW	E	SE	NW	W	NE	S
Earth Punishment	SW	N	NE	W	S	SE	E	NW

Sitting Direction	1	2	3	4	6	7	8	9
Earth Punishment	2	1	8	7	9	4	3	6

Example

Building has Sitting Direction N
The trigram or the number of the N in the Earlier Heaven is in the Later Heaven in the SW, which is the Earth Punishment Position.

Building has Sitting Direction SW
The trigram or the number of the SW in the Later Heaven is in the Earlier Heaven in the N, which is the Earth Punishment Position.

Building has Sitting Direction E
The trigram or the number of the E in the Later Heaven is in the Earlier Heaven in the NE, which is the Earth Punishment Position.

Building has Sitting Direction SE
The trigram or the number of the SE in the Earlier Heaven is in the Later Heaven in the W, which is the Earth Punishment Position.

Building has Sitting Direction NW

The trigram or the number of the NW in the Later Heaven is in the Earlier Heaven in the S, which is the Earth Punishment Position.

Building has Sitting Direction W

The trigram or the number of the W in the Later Heaven is in the Earlier Heaven in the SE, which is the Earth Punishment Position.

Building has Sitting Direction NE

The trigram or the number of the NE in the Earlier Heaven is in the Later Heaven in the E, which is the Earth Punishment Position.

Building has Sitting Direction S

The trigram or the number of the S in the Earlier Heaven is in the Later Heaven in the NW, which is the Earth Punishment Position.

Courtyard Robber Water Position

This formula is based on the Later Heaven arrangement of energies and the Later Heaven harmony feature. No Time Factor involved.

Any objects in the Courtyard Robber directions (which are the Facing Directions) causing destructive energy (cha chi) will bring misfortune. Even water flowing directly from these directions has a destructive influence on fortunes and health. However, when water comes from the Courtyard Robber direction and the Facing Star in the Facing Palace is timely, it is said to increase fortunes during the timely period.

Later Heaven Sitting Directions

Sitting Direction	N	SW	E	SE	NW	W	NE	S
Courtyard Robber	S	NE	W	NW	SE	E	SW	N

Sitting Direction	1	2	3	4	6	7	8	9
Courtyard Robber	9	8	7	6	4	3	2	1

Example

Building has Sitting Direction N
In the Later Heaven harmony feature the number of the N combines with the number of the opposite direction S to the sum of 10. This opposite direction is the Courtyard Robber Direction.

Building has Sitting Direction SW
In the Later Heaven harmony feature the number of the SW combines with the number of the opposite direction NE to the sum of 10. This opposite direction is the Courtyard Robber Direction.

Building has Sitting Direction E
In the Later Heaven harmony feature the number of the E combines with the number of the opposite direction W to the sum of 10. This opposite direction is the Courtyard Robber Direction.

Building has Sitting Direction SE

In the Later Heaven harmony feature the number of the SE combines with the number of the opposite direction NW to the sum of 10. This opposite direction is the Courtyard Robber Direction.

Building has Sitting Direction NW

In the Later Heaven harmony feature the number of the NW combines with the number of the opposite direction SE to the sum of 10. This opposite direction is the Courtyard Robber Direction.

Building has Sitting Direction W

In the Later Heaven harmony feature the number of the W combines with the number of the opposite direction E to the sum of 10. This opposite direction is the Courtyard Robber Direction.

Building has Sitting Direction NE

In the Later Heaven harmony feature the number of the NE combines with the number of the opposite direction SW to the sum of 10. This opposite direction is the Courtyard Robber Direction.

Building has Sitting Direction S

In the Later Heaven harmony feature the number of the S combines with the number of the opposite direction N to the sum of 10. This opposite direction is the Courtyard Robber Direction.

Visitor - Water Position

This formula is based on the Earlier and Later Heaven interaction and the Later Heaven harmony features. No Time Factor involved.

When water comes from these directions it is said to be inauspicious for male members of the family, but auspicious for female members and male members of the extended family, such as stepsons, son-in laws, adopted sons and nephews.

Later Heaven Sitting Directions

Sitting Direction	N	SW	E	SE	NW	W	NE	S
Visitor Direction	E	NW	SE	S	SW	NE	N	W

Sitting Direction	1	2	3	4	6	7	8	9
Visitor Direction	3	6	4	9	2	8	1	3

Examples

Building has Sitting Direction N
In the Later Heaven the trigram or the number of the N has its harmony feature in the S. This trigram or number of the S is in the Earlier Heaven in the E, which is the Visitor Direction.

Building has Sitting Direction SW
In the Later Heaven the trigram or the number of the SW has its harmony feature in the NE. This trigram or number of the NE is in the Earlier Heaven in the NW, which is the Visitor Direction.

Building has Sitting Direction E
In the Later Heaven the trigram or the number of the E has its harmony feature in the W. This trigram or number of the W is in the Earlier Heaven in the SE, which is the Visitor Direction.

Building has Sitting Direction SE

In the Later Heaven the trigram or the number of the SE has its harmony feature in the NW. This trigram or number of the NW is in the Earlier Heaven in the S, which is the Visitor Direction.

Building has Sitting Direction NW

In the Later Heaven the trigram or the number of the NW has its harmony feature in the SE. This trigram or number of the SE is in the Earlier Heaven in the SW, which is the Visitor Direction.

Building has Sitting Direction W

In the Later Heaven the trigram or the number of the W has its harmony feature in the E. This trigram or number of the E is in the Earlier Heaven in the NE which is the Visitor Direction.

Building has Sitting Direction NE

In the Later Heaven the trigram or the number of the NE has its harmony feature in the SW. This trigram or number of the SW is in the Earlier Heaven in the N, which is the Visitor Direction.

Building has Sitting Direction S

In the Later Heaven the trigram or the number of the S has its harmony feature in the N. This trigram or number of the N is in the Earlier Heaven in the W, which is the Visitor Direction.

Guest – Water Position

This formula is based on the Earlier and Later Heaven interaction and the Earlier Heaven harmony features. No Time Factor involved.

When water comes from these directions it is said to be inauspicious for male members of the family, but auspicious for female members and male members of the extended family, such as stepsons, son-in laws, adopted sons and nephews.

Later Heaven Sitting Directions

Sitting Direction	N	SW	E	SE	NW	W	NE	S
Guest Direction	NW	E	N	NE	W	S	SE	SW

Sitting Direction	1	2	3	4	6	7	8	9
Guest Direction	6	3	1	8	7	9	4	2

Examples

Building has Sitting Direction N
In the Earlier Heaven the trigram or the number of the N combines to perfect harmony of yin and yang with the trigram or number of the S, which in the Later Heaven is in the NW, which is the Guest Direction.

Building has Sitting Direction SW
In the Earlier Heaven the trigram or the number of the SW combines to perfect harmony of yin and yang with the trigram or number of the NE, which in the Later Heaven is in the E, which is the Guest Direction.

Building has Sitting Direction E
In the Earlier Heaven the trigram or the number of the E combines to perfect harmony of yin and yang with the trigram or number of the W, which in the Later Heaven is in the N, which is the Guest Direction.

Building has Sitting Direction SE

in the Earlier Heaven The trigram or the number of the SE combines to perfect harmony of yin and yang with the trigram or number of the NW which in the Later Heaven is in the NE, which is the Guest Direction.

Building has Sitting Direction NW

In the Earlier Heaven the trigram or the number of the NW in the Earlier Heaven combines to perfect harmony of yin and yang with the trigram or number of the SE which in the Later Heaven is in the W, which is the Guest Direction.

Building has Sitting Direction W

In the Earlier Heaven the trigram or the number of the W combines to perfect harmony of yin and yang with the trigram or number of the E, which in the Later Heaven is in the S, which is the Guest Direction.

Building has Sitting Direction NE

In the Earlier Heaven the trigram or the number of the NE combines to perfect harmony of yin and yang with the trigram or number of the SW which in the Later Heaven is in the SE, which is the Guest Direction.

Building has Sitting Direction S

In the Earlier Heaven the trigram or the number of the S combines to perfect harmony of yin and yang with the trigram or number of the N which in the Later Heaven is in the SW, which is the Guest Direction.

Auxiliary Water Position

Based on the interaction of the Earlier and Later Heaven and the Harmony Features of the two heavens. No Time Factor involved.

Water in these directions supports health and good relationships. A collection of water, such as a pool supports the accumulation of wealth.

Later Heaven Sitting Directions

Sitting Directions	N	SW	E	SE	NW	W	NE	S
Auxiliary Trigram	NE	S	SW	E	N	NW	W	SE

Sitting Directions	1	2	3	4	6	7	8	9
Auxiliary Trigram	8	9	2	3	1	6	7	4

Examples

Building has Sitting Direction N

The N in the Earlier Heaven has a trigram or number, which is in the SW of the Later Heaven and combines with the number of the NE to the sum of 10. The NE is the Auxiliary Direction.

Building has Sitting Direction SW

The SW in the Later Heaven has a trigram, which is in the N of the Earlier Heaven and combines with the trigram of the S to perfect harmony of yin and yang. The S is the Auxiliary Direction.

Building has Sitting Direction E

The E in the Later Heaven has a trigram, which is in the NE of the Earlier Heaven and combines with the trigram of the SW to perfect harmony of yin and yang. The SW is the Auxiliary Direction.

Building has Sitting Direction SE

The SE in the Earlier Heaven has a trigram or number, which is in the W of the Later Heaven and combines with the number of the E to the sum of 10. The E is the Auxiliary Direction.

Building has Sitting Direction NW

The NW in the Later Heaven has a trigram, which is in the S of the Earlier Heaven and combines with the trigram of the N to to perfect harmony of yin and yang. The N is the Auxiliary Direction.

Building has Sitting Direction W

The W in the Later Heaven has a trigram, which is in the SE of the Earlier Heaven and combines with the trigram of the NW to perfect harmony of yin and yang. The NW is the Auxiliary Direction.

Building has Sitting Direction NE

The NE in the Earlier Heaven has a trigram or number, which is in the E of the Later Heaven and combines with the number of the W to the sum of 10. The W is the Auxiliary Direction.

Building has Sitting Direction S

The S in the Earlier Heaven has a trigram or number, which is in the NW of the Later Heaven and combines with the number of the SE to the sum of 10. The SE is the Auxiliary Direction.

Five Ghosts carry Money

A Formula based on the Harmony Features of the Earlier and Later Heaven Arrangement of Energies and on the Interaction of the two Heavens to enhance Wealth.

The Formula comes in two Parts

1. **The Mountain Dragon and**
2. **The Water Dragon and it uses**

The Eight Trigram Groups of Directions

Trigram Direction	Included Directions	Trigram Direction	Included Directions
Qian	Qian, Jia	NW	NW2, E1
Kun	Kun, Yi	SW	SW2, E3
Gen	Gen, Bing	NE	NE2, S1
Xun	Xun, Xin	SE	SE2, W3
Kan	Zi, Gui, Shen, Chen	N	N2, N3, SW3 SE1
Li	Wu, Ren, Yin, Xu	S	S2, N1, NE3, NW1
Zhen	Geng, Hai, Mao, Wei	E	W1, NW3, E2, SW1
Dui	Ding, Si, You, Chou	W	S3, SE3, W2, NE1

Assigning the 9 Stars of the Eight Trigram Groups to the 24 Compass Directions (Mountains)
The Mountain Dragon

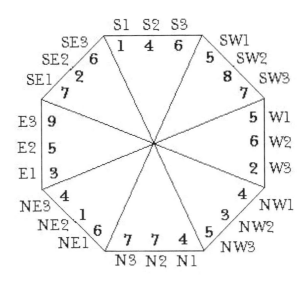

Change Trigram

A Mountain Dragon is obtained by changing one line of each of the eight trigrams starting with the trigram to which the Sitting Direction belongs (see list of Eight Trigram-Groups of Directions).

The lines are changed from yin to yang or from yang to yin applying a certain sequence. The trigrams altered by this process are then accorded certain numbers. The groups of directions represented by trigrams, which are given the numbers 2 and 5, combine their energies to a perfect balance of yin and yang, which is most auspicious. Number 2 is said to be wealth enhancing, if certain conditions are met.

How to create a Mountain Dragon

Determine the Sitting Direction (Mountain). Find out to which group the Sitting Direction belongs. Take the trigram under which the Sitting Direction is included (see list of Eight Trigram-Groups of Directions). Start with this trigram changing the upper then the middle and thereafter the lower line, if yang into yin or if yin into yang and continue changing lines in the sequence stipulated. The Sequence of changing the lines for Mountain Dragon is:

Upper-Middle-Lower-Middle-Upper-Middle-Lower-Middle

We start with changing the upper line of the trigram under which the Sitting Direction is listed. Thereafter we change the middle line of the trigram and then the lower line from yin to yang or from yang to yin and continue that way with the rest of the trigrams applying the stipulated sequence of changing lines for the Mountain Dragon.

Example

The Sitting Direction S3 belongs to the group of the trigram W. We begin changing lines starting with the trigram for the W. Numbers starting from 1 to 8 are then assigned to the trigrams of the Mountain Dragon. The trigrams listed under the numbers 2 (trigram for the S) and 5 (trigram for the N) when combined give a perfect balance of yin and yang.

When the directions listed under the trigram of number 5 are either Facing Directions or directions of main doors, the formula says that "Five Ghosts" are at the door. This is one of the conditions of the formula. When the directions listed under the trigram of number 2 have water flowing from there, the formula says "Carry Money". When both of these conditions are given, it is "Five Ghosts Carry Money".

List of Mountain Dragons for the Eight Trigrams of Sitting Directions

Trigram Directions		S	SW	W	NW	N	NE	E	SE
Trigrams under which Sitting Directions are included		☱	☷	☳	☰	☵	☶	☲	☴
Upper line	1								
Middle line	2								
Lower line	3								
Middle line	4								
Upper line	5								
Middle line	6								
Lower line	7								
Middle line	8								

The Water Dragon Change Trigram

A Water Dragon also is obtained by changing one line of each of the eight trigrams. The Water Dragon is based on the trigram of number 5 of the Mountain Dragon. Starting with the trigram of number 5 of the Mountain Dragon the lines are changed from yin to yang or from yang to yin applying a certain sequence different from the sequence applied to the Mountain Dragon. The sequence of changing lines for the Water Dragon is:

Middle-Lower-Middle-Upper-Middle-Lower-Middle-Upper

The trigrams altered by this process are then accorded the numbers 6, 7, 5, 1, 2, 3, 4 and 8.

The trigram of number 2 of the Water Dragon combined with the trigram of number 5 of the Mountain Dragon make a perfect balance of yin and yang. The groups of directions represented by trigrams which are the number 2 of the Water Dragon and number 5 of the Mountain Dragon combine their energies to a perfect balance of yin and yang which is most auspicious and wealth enhancing.

List of Water Dragons for the Eight Trigrams of Number 5 of the Mountain Dragons

Trigram Directions		S	SW	W	NW	N	NE	E	SE
Trigrams under which Facing Directions are included		☷	☵	☳	☰	☴	☶	☱	☲
Middle line	6								
Lower line	7								
Middle line	5								
Upper line	1								
Middle line	2								
Lower line	3								
Middle line	4								
Upper line	8								

171

Comparing Mountain Dragon with Water Dragon

As you will have noticed, when comparing the Trigrams of number 2 of the Mountain Dragon with the trigrams of number 2 of the Water Dragon, they are in fact identical.

For the formula "Five Ghosts Carry Money" it is therefore not necessary to make a Water Dragon to obtain the directions of the number 2 trigrams. They can simply be taken from the Mountain Dragon.

Let us now demystify the Formula

Harmony Features of the Earlier and Later Heaven

Arrangements of Energies

**Earlier Heaven
Arrangement of Energie**

**Later Heaven
Arrangement of Energies**

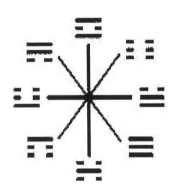

We have to ask ourselves

What is the central idea of the formula?

The central idea is the perfect balance of yin and yang as seen in the opposite directions of the Earlier Heaven arrangement of energies.

The Earlier Heaven Harmony Feature

The opposing directions of the Earlier Heaven arrangement of energies when combined make three yang and three yin lines. This is perfect harmony of yin and yang energies and is most fortunate.

The trigrams of number 2 and number 5 of the Mountain Dragon display this same feature of harmony. The energy of number 5 enters the building through the door or from the Facing Direction. The energy of number 2 is carried into the building by the flow of water. Both energies combine in perfect harmony of yin and yang forces inside the building.

Depending on the nature of their energies in relation to the Sitting Direction on which the Mountain Dragon is based, these energy combinations are enhancing wealth.

Where do we find this Balance of Yin and Yang in the Later Heaven?

The Earlier Heaven arrangement of energies is the underlying reality of the world in perfect harmony and stillness.

The Later Heaven arrangement of energies represents the world of changes as we perceive and know the world in which we live.

Perfect harmony of yin and yang in the Later Heaven arrangement is found in the combination of the trigrams

SW combined with NW
W combined with NE
E combined with SE
S combined with N

The Later Heaven Harmony Feature

The opposing directions of the Earlier Heaven arrangement of energies when combined always make a sum of 10, which is very auspicious

Later Heaven in numbers

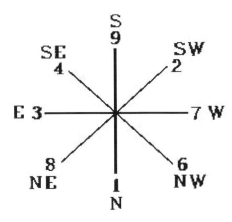

The Harmony Feature of the Later Heaven is also found in the opposite directions, which always add up to the sum of 10. This feature is found in **The Combination of 10** special Flying Star chart. It creates harmony of the energies of the Earth Base and the Facing or Mountain Stars in all the 9 palaces.

The Interaction of the Two Heavens

The Five Ghosts Carry Money Water Formula is based on the trigrams of the Later Heaven Sitting Direction of a building and the harmony feature of the Earlier Heaven to determine the direction of the Later Heaven from which water should flow to enhance wealth.

"Five Ghosts Carry Money" is a very powerful water formula because it is based on the harmony features of the Earlier and the Later Heaven and on the interaction of the Two Heavens. It is one of the well-guarded secrets of authentic Chinese Feng Shui. The formula is independent of any time period. Its application is also independent of the nature of the Stars, which are present in the 9 Palaces of a building.

Table of Sitting Directions with their Facing or Door Directions and the Directions of Water Flow.

This Table contains the whole of the "Five Ghosts Carry Money" Formula (5/2)

Sitting Directions	5 Facing / Door Directions	2 Directions of Water Flow
N2, N3, SW3, SE1	W2, S3, SE3, NE1	NE2, S1
S2, N1, NE3, NW1	NE2, S1	W2, S3, SE3, NE1
W1, NW3, E2, SW1	SW2, E3	NW2, E1
S3, SE3, W2, NE1	N2, N3, SW3, SE1	S2, N1, NE3, NW1
NW2, E1	SE2, W3	W1, NW3, E2, SW1
SW2, E3	W1, NW3, E2, SW1	SE2, W3
NE2, S1	S2, N1, NE3, NW1	N2, N3, SW3, SE1
SE2, W3	NW2, E1	SW2, E3

The Relationship of the Directions listed under the Numbers

5 / 2

The Sitting Directions included under the trigram N
Have under number 5 directions, which are included under the trigram W and have under number 2 directions, which are included under the trigram NE.
The trigrams for W and NE in the Later Heaven relate to each other in the Earlier Heaven in perfect harmony of yin and yang.

The Sitting Directions included under the trigram S
Have under number 5 directions, which are included under the trigram NE and have under number 2 directions, which are included under the trigram W.

The trigrams for NE and W in the Later Heaven relate to each other in the Earlier Heaven in perfect harmony of yin and yang.

The Sitting Directions included under the trigram E

Have under number 5 directions, which are included under the trigram SW and have under number 2 directions, which are included under the trigram NW.

The trigrams for SW and NW in the Later Heaven relate to each other in the Earlier Heaven in perfect harmony of yin and yang

.

The Sitting Directions included under the trigram W

Have under number 5 directions, which are included under the trigram N and have under number 2 directions, which are included under the trigram S.

The trigrams for N and S relate to each other in the Earlier and Later Heaven in perfect harmony of yin and yang.

The Sitting Directions included under the trigram NW

Have under number 5 directions, which are included under the trigram SE and have under number 2 directions, which are included under the trigram E.

The trigrams for SE and E in the Later Heaven relate to each other in the Earlier Heaven in perfect harmony of yin and yang.

The Sitting Directions included under the trigram SW

Have under number 5 directions, which are included under the trigram E and have under number 2 directions, which are included under the trigram SE.

The trigrams for SE and E in the Later Heaven relate to each other in the Earlier Heaven in perfect harmony of yin and yang.

The Sitting Directions included under the trigram NE

Have under number 5 directions, which are included under the trigram S and have under number 2 directions, which are included under the trigram N.

The trigrams for S and N in the Later and the Earlier Heaven relate to each other in perfect harmony of yin and yang.

The Sitting Directions included under the trigram SE

Have under number 5 directions, which are included under the trigram NW and have under number 2 directions, which are included under the trigram SW.

The trigrams for NW and SW in the Later Heaven relate to each other in the Earlier Heaven in perfect harmony of yin and yang.

Five Ghosts Carry Money Formula in Graphics

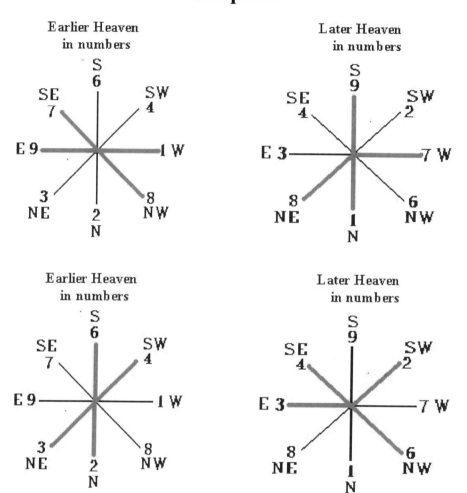

Earlier Heaven Harmony Features

When looking at the graphics above you can see that the 8 trigrams make four pairs of two Sitting Directions each, which relate to each other in perfect harmony of yin and yang. Each pair of Sitting Directions shares the same trigrams of the directions of the numbers 2 and 5.

The Relationship of the Sitting Directions to the Directions
listed under Numbers 2 and 5 of the Mountain Dragon

Directions of the Numbers 2 and 5 are red. Sitting Directions are green.

Sitting Directions N=1 and S=9

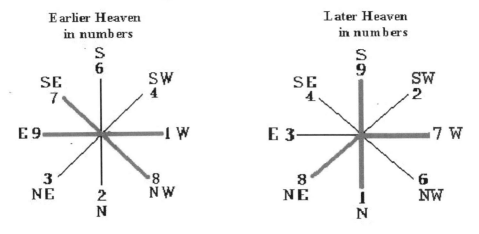

Sitting Direction N=1

The trigram of the Sitting Direction in the Later Heaven is in the N. The same trigram is found in the W direction of the Earlier Heaven, which is the direction of number 5 of the Mountain Dragon in the Later Heaven.

Sitting Direction S=9

The trigram of the Sitting Direction in the Later Heaven is in the S. The Earlier Heaven has in the S a trigram, which in the Later Heaven is found in the NW. The NW in the Earlier Heaven has a trigram, which in the Later Heaven is the number 5 of the Mountain Dragon.

Sitting Direction NE=8 and W=7

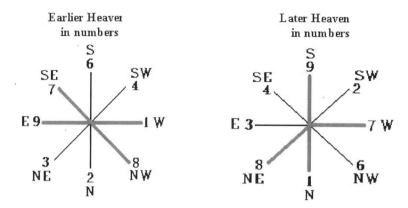

Sitting Direction NE=8

The trigram of the Sitting Direction in the Later Heaven is in the NE. The same trigram is found in the NW direction of the Earlier Heaven.

The trigram of the NW direction of the Later Heaven is found in the S direction of the Earlier Heaven. The S direction of the Later Heaven is the direction of number 5 of the Mountain Dragon.

Sitting Direction W=7

The trigram of the Sitting Direction in the Later Heaven is in the W. The Direction W in the Earlier Heaven has a trig ram, which in the Later Heaven is found in the N and which is the Number 5 of the Mountain Dragon.

Sitting Direction SW=2 and NW=6

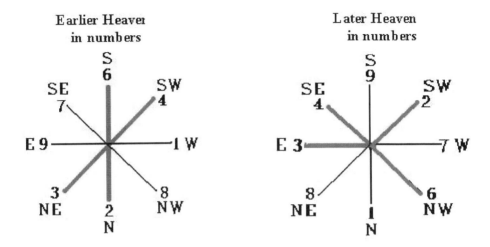

Earlier Heaven in numbers

Later Heaven in numbers

Sitting Direction SW=2

The trigram of the Sitting Direction in the Later Heaven is in the SW. The Direction SW in the Earlier Heaven has a trig ram, which in the Later Heaven is found in the SE and which is the Number 2 of the Mountain Dragon.

Sitting Direction NW=6

The trigram of the Sitting Direction in the Later Heaven is in the NW. The direction NW in the Earlier Heaven has a trigram, which in the Later Heaven is found in the NE. The NE in the Earlier Heaven has a trigram which in the Later Heaven is in the E and which is the Number 2 of the Mountain Dragon..

Sitting Directions SE=4 and E=3

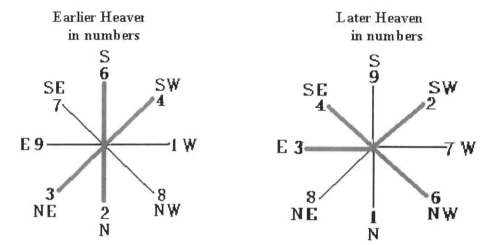

Earlier Heaven in numbers

Later Heaven in numbers

Sitting Direction SE=4

The trigram of the Sitting Direction in the Later Heaven is in the SE. The same trigram is found in the SW in the Earlier Heaven. The SW in the Later Heaven is the direction of number 2 of the Mountain Dragon.

Sitting Direction E=3

The trigram of the Sitting Direction in the Later Heaven is in the E. The same trigram is found in the Earlier Heaven in the NE. The NE in the Later Heaven has a trigram, which is found in the Earlier Heaven in the NW. The NW in the Later Heaven is the direction of number 2 of the Mountain Dragon.

The Formula can be used for Buildings and for Burial Sites.

Burial sites

Burial sites are marked by their Sitting Directions, which are usually the directions of the Headstone. They do not generally have a distinct Facing Direction. In applying the formula we have to rely therefore on the Sitting Direction.

The method
Create a Mountain Dragon by changing lines starting with the trigram under which the Sitting Direction is included.
Number 5 of the Mountain Dragon will be the direction for a door or the Facing Direction. Since this direction will be open land in a burial site with no marked direction from which energy enters, we have to use water flowing from that direction to carry energy to the site.
Number 2 of the Mountain Dragon will be the direction from which water is to flow towards the site to enhance wealth prospects.
The energies of the numbers 5 and 2 directed to the site by the flow of water will combine to a perfect balance of three yin and three yang lines which is most auspicious and means Ghosts are at the door carrying money.

Buildings

Buildings generally have well noticeable Facing Directions, which are the directions from which maximum yang energy enters. These are mostly the directions of main doors or that front of a building, which has the largest exposure to outside energy, which is marked by a strong yang quality.
The method
As prescribed in the formula, we have to create a Mountain Dragon based on the Sitting Direction.
Number 5 of the Mountain Dragon will then be the Facing Direction or the direction of the main door from which energy enters the building. Based on the direction of number 5 we have to create a Water Dragon by changing lines starting with the trigram of number 5 of the Mountain Dragon.
Number 2 of the Water Dragon will then be the direction from which water should flow towards the building carrying the energy, which is able to enhance wealth prospects.
The energies of the numbers 5 and 2 directed to the site by the flow of water and from the Facing Direction or door will combine to a perfect balance of three yin and three yang lines which is most auspicious and means Ghosts are at the door carrying money.

As we have seen earlier the directions of number 2 of the Mountain and the Water Dragon are identical

The Formula speaks of Number 5 of the Mountain Dragon as being the Facing Direction or the Direction of the Main Door

As you can see below, only the Sitting Directions given in red have under number 5 of the Mountain Dragon Facing Directions which are 180 ° apart from the Sitting Direction.

Sitting Direction	No.5 (Facing Direction)	No.2 (Water)
N2,N3,SW3,SE1	W2,S3,SE3,NE1	NE2,S1
S2,N1,NE3,NW1	NE2,S1	W2,S3,SE3,NE1
E2,W1,NW3,SW1	SW2,E3	NW2,E1
W2,S3,SE3,NE1	N2,N3,SW3,SE1	S2,N1,NE3,NW1
NW2,E1	SE2,W3	E2,W1,NW3,SW1
SW2,E3	E2,W1,NW3,SW1	SE2,W3
NE2,S1	S2,N1,NE3,NW1	N2,N3,SW3,SE1
SE2,W3	NW2,E1	SW2,E3

Are we to use the Facing Direction of a Building or the Direction of number 5 of the Mountain Dragon ?

Applying the formula on a building we can be in doubt if the direction of number 5 of the Mountain Dragon or the actual Facing Direction should be used to create a Water Dragon to find the direction of number 2.

After all only 6 of the 24 Sitting Directions have Facing Directions, which are identical with the directions of number 5 of the Mountain Dragon.

There are some Parts in the Formula, which need Investigation

To find the direction from which water should flow the formula uses two methods

1.) For Burial Sites the formula uses only the Mountain Dragon
2.) For Buildings the formula uses the Mountain and the Water Dragon

The direction of number 2 from which water should flow, obtained by both methods, are however identical. This leads to the questions:

- Is the method of the Water Dragon to find the direction of number 2 in case of a building obsolete?

What is the point of using the Water Dragon for a building, when the direction of the water flow can also be obtained from the Mountain Dragon?
My answer is: The method of using the Water Dragon for a building to find the direction of number 2 is superfluous.

- Need we use the Mountain Dragon for a building to find the direction of number 5 or could we use the Water Dragon based on the trigram of the actual Facing Direction to arrive at the direction of number 2?

The relationship of the Sitting Direction to the directional energies of number 5 and 2 determines the wealth enhancing quality of their yin/yang harmony.
These two directional energies have to enter the building to be effective. This happens through the Facing Direction, a door or by the flow of water.
My answer is therefore: In case of a building we should not use the Water Dragon based on the actual Facing Direction, but the Mountain Dragon to find the directions of number 5 and number 2.

How important are Features in the External Environment

All Feng Shui schools agree that it is important to have external features in the environment to support the internal energies of a building, Some schools go to the extreme by saying that in case the external features are missing or do not support the internal energies, the internal energies are only mere numbers and will not have any effect.
This is a very serious statement. Since our modern urban living conditions do not allow alterations of the external environment. All buildings not having the proper external support for their internal energies would be doomed and cannot be helped by Feng Shui methods. Schools, which have this extreme

attitude, have in my opinion not understood the basic fundamentals of Feng Shui as yet.

Feng Shui deals with global directional energy. Mountain formations, lakes and rivers as well as man made structures influence the global directional energy in their vicinity, but so does the structure of a building.

A building's construction period and Facing Direction modify the global directional energy inside the building as is evident in the Facing, Mountain and Earth Base Stars.

Feng Shui knows methods to support and manipulate the internal energies of a building and to counteract negative influences caused by features in the external environment.

If a building does not have a door or its Facing Direction in the direction of number 5 of the Mountain Dragon and energy from this direction cannot enter, we can generate the required energy inside the building with water features. By doing so we create conditions internally which are missing externally. The effect will however be much reduced on account of the relatively smaller size of the internal water features. The same applies when we do not have a river flowing from the direction of number 2 in the external environment.

The Five Ghosts Carry Money formula can therefore be applied to any building.

What to do if the formula doesn't work?

When done correctly the formula will always work. If it doesn't we may have made one or more of the following mistakes:

1. The angles of the direction of the water flow are not correct.
2. The Sitting Direction is not correct. To determine the correct Sitting Direction or Facing Direction can at times be one of the most difficult tasks.

Heavenly Doctor Water Formula

This formula is disclosed and published here for the very first time.

This formula is also based on the Mountain Dragon and the yin / yang harmony feature of the Earlier Heaven and is said to promote good health and relationships.

The Combination of the numbers 8 and 3

The directions under number 8 of the Mountain Dragon (see: Five Ghosts carry Money Formula) are the Sitting Directions, which are generally held to be responsible for good health and good relationships. In combination with the directions under number 3

perfect harmony of yin and yang is created. Water flowing from the directions of number 3 will therefore carry energy, which in combination with the energy of the Sitting Direction will produce forces stimulating good health and excellent relationships.

Formula 8/3

8 Sitting Directions	3 Directions of Water Flow
N2, N3, SW3, SE1	S2, N1, NE3, NW1
S2, N1, NE3, NW1	N2, N3, SW3, SE1
W1, NW3, E2, SW1	SE2, W3
S3, SE3, W2, NE1	NE2, S1
NW2, E1	SW2, E3
SW2, E3	NW2, E1
NE2, S1	S3, SE3, W2, NE1
SE2, W3	W1, NW3, E2, SW1

The Relationship of the Directions listed under the Numbers

8 / 3

The Sitting Directions included under the trigram N

Have under number 3 directions, which are included under the trigram S. The trigrams for N and S in the Later Heaven relate to each other in the Earlier and Later Heaven in perfect harmony of yin and yang.

The Sitting Directions included under the trigram S

Have under number 3 directions, which are included under the trigram N. The trigrams for S and N in the Later Heaven relate to each other in the Earlier and Later Heaven in perfect harmony of yin and yang.

The Sitting Directions included under the trigram E

Have under number 3 directions, which are included under the trigram SE. The trigrams for SE and E in the Later Heaven relate to each other in the Earlier Heaven in perfect harmony of yin and yang.

The Sitting Directions included under the trigram W

Have under number 3 directions, which are included under the trigram NE. The trigrams for W and NE in the Later Heaven relate to each other in the Earlier Heaven in perfect harmony of yin and yang.

The Sitting Directions included under the trigram NW

Have under number 3 directions, which are included under the trigram SW. The trigrams for NW and SW in the Later Heaven relate to each other in the Earlier Heaven in perfect harmony of yin and yang.

The Sitting Directions included under the trigram SW

Have under number 3 directions, which are included under the trigram NW. The trigrams for SW and NW in the Later Heaven relate to each other in the Earlier Heaven in perfect harmony of yin and yang.

The Sitting Directions included under the trigram NE

Have under number 3 directions, which are included under the trigram W. The trigrams for NE and W in the Later Heaven relate to each other in the Earlier Heaven in perfect harmony of yin and yang.

The Sitting Directions included under the trigram SE

Have under number 3 directions, which are included under the trigram E. The trigrams for SE and E in the Later Heaven relate to each other in the Earlier Heaven in perfect harmony of yin and yang.

Change of Period and the Time Factor

In order to see how the directional energies are distributed in a building the Time Factor and the Facing Direction have to be determined. Different schools apply different principles to do so.

The Time Factor

Three systems are in use. Most schools ardently defend their system, claiming it to be the only correct one. Let us compare and analyze the three systems to understand their virtues.

1.) Period of Construction

The Time Factor is determined by the period in which the building was constructed. This method is based on the assumption that the energy of the period in which the building was constructed, becomes part of it. This is comparable to the concept used in astrology, that the energy prevalent at the time of birth determines the physical and mental characteristics and the fate of a human being throughout its entire life.

2.) The Current Period

The Time Factor is determined by the period currently reigning. This method is based on the view that the energy of the presently ruling period is strongest and dominates any other energy, which may have been captured in the building at the time of construction (or occupancy).

3.) Move in Date

The Time Factor is determined by the period during which the present occupants moved into the building. This concept is based on the three lines of the trigrams for the eight directions of the Earlier and Later Heaven arrangement of energies. The three lines of the trigrams symbolize "Heaven", "Earth" and "Man". Some schools apply this symbolism to the energy of buildings, assuming that the energy depends on these three factors. To them the Move-in Date of the present occupants is the time when the "Man" part of the energy entered and made the building's energy complete. They therefore believe that the Move-in Date determines the Time Factor. This method is controversial, as we will see later.

How the Different Systems deal with a Change of Period

Period of Construction

The Period of Construction determines the Time Factor independent of any period, which may be ruling at present. This Time Factor remains the same throughout all nine periods.

Schools, which follow this system, believe in the waxing and waning of the Earth Base or Time Energy. That is to say, the level of energy of Earth Base Stars is not the same throughout the 9 Periods (see: The Timeliness of Energy). For example, the Earth Base energy of a building constructed during period 6 will be good in period 8, but the Earth Base energy of a period 7 building is failing in period 8. When the energy of the Earth Base or Time Star is "failing" or "death" it is advised to remedy this energy deficiency.

1. Buildings having "The Three-Combination Charts", which can take in the strong period energy of all 9 periods (see: The Three-Combination Charts) receive the strong period energy of all periods automatically and nothing needs to be done.

2. Buildings having a " Seven Star Robbery Chart " can take in automatically the strong period energy of the six periods, which have the numbers of the two Parent Trigrams that constitute the chart (see: The Seven Star Robbery Charts). In such a case nothing needs to be done.

3. The method of "Inviting the Energy of a Different Period" is a well-known technique applied when a new period has started, which is different from the construction period of the building and the Earth Base energy turns failing or death. In such a case the Facing Star having the number of the new period has to be activated (see: Inviting the Energy of a Different Period).

4. In case the chart based on the period of construction has a formation known as "Jailed Star", which prevents the energy of the new period to enter the building, one should first apply the remedy (see: Jailed Period Star) and thereafter use the method of "Inviting the Energy of a Different Period".

Curing the "Jailed Period Star" formation by changing the Facing Direction is the best way to overcome the problem. This may on the other hand not always be possible.

5. The method of "Inviting the Energy of a Different Period" can also be applied when the Earth Base energy is still good in a new period. This is often done in order to benefit from the ruling period's high level of energy. It may however not always be advisable to do so. When the energies of the new period's chart conflict to much with the energies of the Construction Period's chart unwelcome consequences can occur, which are better avoided.

The Current Period

Guided by the generally acknowledged view that the ruling period's energy is strongest and has the greatest impact and therefore takes priority over any other energy, some schools make a new chart for the building based on the number of the new period. For example, a period 7 building with a Facing Direction N3 is changed into a period 8 building with Facing Direction N3.

While everyone agrees on the dominating strength of the ruling period's energy, we also have to consider, if the new period's energy is able to enter the building. Schools using the Current Period as Time Factor however do not pay any attention to this problem relying fully on the dominating strength of the new period's energy.

Move-in Date

The Time Factor is based on the date on which the present occupants moved in. Residents who have moved in during period 7 can change the building's energies from period 7 to period 8 by keeping the building vacant for 100 days and then move in again in period 8. In keeping with the rationale of this method the 100 days vacancy required to change the energies from one period to the next one should also be applied when for example new residents are moving in during a new period. This however is strangely not seen to be necessary.

When new residents move in during a new period, the general practice is that the Move-in Date of the new residents is understood to determine the Time Factor. In such a case the 100 days vacancy is not required and the building is deemed to have automatically the energies of the new period. This is even so when the former residents, who had occupied the building since the earlier period, had vacated it only a few days earlier and for that reason the "Man" part of the building's energy was never missing.

From the above we can understand that the Move-in Date method is not consistent in its application and is in fact most of the time identical with the "Current Period" method.

It is also difficult to make out why the advocates of the "Move-in Date" system concern themselves with the "Jailed Period Stars" and the "Seven Star Robbery Formations", when all it takes to allow the strong energies of a new period to enter a building, would be a vacancy of 100 days. Surely this is a small price to pay for 20 years of strong period energies.

Summary

Considering the underlying principles of all three methods, the "Period of Construction" and the "Current Period" method are based on concepts, which can be rationally comprehended. Contrary to this the method of the "Move-in Date" in its application appears to be identical with the "Current Period" method and nothing more. Since the 100 days vacancy concept is applied inconsistently as we have seen, it doesn't make much sense either.

Comparing the "Period of Construction" and the "Current Period" method we see that both are sharing the idea that the ruling period's energy is strongest. The "Current Period" method is entirely based on it overruling all other considerations.

The "Period of Construction" method takes a more differentiated view and considers how the energy of a period other than the "Period of Construction" can enter a building. It thereby acknowledges that apart of the construction period's energies, the energies of a currently ruling period can be present in a building.

As the strongest energies in a building will have the strongest impact on the residents we have to ask ourselves which energy is stronger? The energy of the current Period is certainly the strongest as such but, depending on how it can enter, may not be the strongest energy once inside a building.

In case of a "Jailed Period Star" the energy of the current period will not be able to enter the building at all, being blocked out by the way the Construction Period's energies are distributed in the chart.

In case of a "Three-Combination Chart" and a " Seven Star Robbery Chart " in which the Current Period's number is part of the two Parent Trigrames, the Current Period's energy can enter unobstructed by virtue of the charts.

In case the method of "Inviting the New Period's Energy" is employed, the new period's energy will enter the building, but to a lesser degree.

It is advisable not to ignore the Current Period's energy when we can assume it has entered the building, but not knowing which of the energies is stronger; we should use the method of "Multiple Charts" (see Multiple Charts).

When using "Multiple Charts" we should first determine which countermeasures and enhancers are to be applied to suit the requirements of each chart. Thereafter we compare the countermeasures and enhancers needed for both charts and where not in agreement, but conflicting, decide for those of the "Period of Construction Chart". The requirements of the Construction Period Chart are always to be given prominence.

Example

Period 7 Facing N 2/3

	SE	S	SW	
	1 4 **6**	6 8 **2**	8 6 **4**	
E	9 5 **5**	2 -3 **7**	4 1 **9**	**W**
	5 9 **1**	7 7 **3**	3 2 **8**	
	NE	N	NW	

Period 8 Facing N 2/3

	SE	S	SW	
	4 3 **7**	8 8 **3**	6 1 **5**	
E	5 2 **6**	-3 4 **8**	1 6 **1**	**W**
	9 7 **2**	7 9 **4**	2 5 **9**	
	NE	N	NW	

N Palace in period 7 chart requires water as countermeasure to break up the harmful 7/3 combinations. In period 8 chart countermeasures are not required, but a water feature will do no harm as it reduces the number 7, enhances the number 4 and makes perfect harmony of yin and yang with number 9.

NE Palace in period 7 chart needs water as countermeasure to combat Facing Star number 9 which enhances star number 5. In period 8 chart the combination 2/7 represents the fire element, which together with star number 9 enhances the earth element of the NE which is desirable, but because of its strength may cause fire in that area. A water countermeasure may therefore be needed.

E Palace in period 7 chart requires metal as countermeasure to combat the double 5. In the period 8 chart also metal is required as countermeasure for the numbers 2 and 5.

SE Palace in period 7 chart does not require any countermeasure, but water will enhance the good energy combination favorably. In the period 8 chart water will be a very good countermeasure for the negative energy of number 7 while enhancing the energies of the numbers 3 and 4 making perfect harmony of yin and yang.

S Palace in period 7 chart will benefit greatly from water or the metal element of No.7 (Calabash). In the period 8 chart water will enhance the exceptionally good energy combination 3/8 and should be applied.

SW Palace period 7 chart needs no countermeasure or enhancer. In period 8 chart metal countermeasure is required which will not interfere with the energy combination of the period 7 chart.

W Palace period 7 chart needs no countermeasure, but metal can enhance to some extend and bring good results. The energy situation in the period 8 chart, on account of the 6/1 combination which reduces the metal element of the W, can lead to problems with children while it is likely to enhance income. A wood countermeasure (plant) will reduce both affects of the 6/1 combination and would not interfere with the energies of the period 7 chart.

NW Palace of the period 7 chart metal element of number 6 (wind chime) is needed to combat number 2, which will create harmony of yin and yang and the wholesome combination of 6/8. In period 8 chart metal will reduce the malevolent energies of the numbers 2 and 5.

Conclusion

As it is our aim to diagnose the energies of our living and working environment in order to manipulate them for our well-being, we have to know what we are dealing with.

There is the energy arrangement of the Later Heaven, the energies of the Facing, the Earth Base, the Mountain, the Annual and the Monthly Stars, which we have to understand and to consider in their interactions.

More often than not this will be an enormous task to perform causing a lot of confusion, uncertainty and doubt. When trying to do a perfect job this is surely going to happen. Looking for help may sometimes not be the answer, which leaves us to rely on our own resources.

The knowledge we have may be extensive, but a method to apply our knowledge may be missing or is excessively complicated.

Considering the interaction of six different energies in each palace, as there are the energies of the Later Heaven, the Facing, Mountain, Earth Base, Annual and Monthly Stars is very complicated and may not lead us anywhere. We therefore should try to use a simplified method.

Basically there are two methods in use. These are:

1. **Main attention is given to the interaction of the Facing and Mountain Stars.** Both stars symbolize the yin / yang duality of the cosmic energy as modified by the time period and the directional exposure (Facing Direction). The Mountain Star is understood to be responsible for health and human relationships and the Facing Star governs wealth and prosperity. Both stars are attributed benevolent or malevolent characteristics depending on their timelines (see: The Timelines of Energy). Even when a star is basically malevolent in nature, when in its own period is seen to be prosperous and therefore benevolent. The support for the Facing and Mountain Stars by features (mountain or water) in the external environment is considered to be essential.

2. **The Facing and the Earth Base Stars are held to carry the strongest energies.** Their character and interaction is therefore seen as causing the strongest results. They have dominating influence on the energy situation in a palace and are therefore considered most important. The energy of the Earth Base Stars is thought of as waxing and waning in different periods, which strengthens or weakens their influence. The character of both stars is not seen as changing. If malevolent they stay malevolent and if benevolent they stay benevolent throughout all periods. The support for the Facing and Mountain Stars by features (mountain or water) in the external environment is not considered to be essential. Apart of the interaction of the stars according to the system of the Five Elements the so-called Additive Effect method is applied, in which the energy level of the stars is considered. A higher level of benevolent energy can outweigh a lower level of malevolent energy.

We may decide for one of the above methods or use both as we may feel is best fitting the situation. The next consideration is where to start.

Always start to analyze the energies of the Facing Palace first, since they are the dominating energies in a building. Then pay attention to the palace in which the main door is found, since the traffic through the door will greatly enhance the energies there. The Center Palace may be next, because its energies will affect every occupant of the building. The rest of the palaces may be done thereafter.

When analyzing the energies of these three palaces look out for Ho Tu number combinations first and break up combinations, if found in the waning positions.

See if there are number combinations relating to certain directions of the Later Heaven such as 3/1 in the W, which is the cause for many descendents or 2/8 (2 being Earth Base and 8 is the Facing Star) in the NW causing tremendous wealth.

The energies of the Later Heaven arrangement have to be considered only in connection with the Ho Tu number combinations and the special number combination.

Use the method of the Additive Effect to determine the overall character of the energies in the palaces.

Look out for the malevolent stars number 2 and 5 and cure them.
This has to be done for all palaces in which stars number 2 and 5 are found. Never use water in palaces having the stars number 2 and 5 except when star number 9 is also present.

Pay attention to the malevolent star number 9. If star number 9 is in company with the stars number 2, 5, 6 and 7 in any of the 9 palaces you have to cure it with water.

Make use of the Host/Guest Relationship of the Stars and the system of the Five Elements to cure or balance the energies of the Earth Base, the Facing and the Mountain Stars as these three stars represent the dominant energies of a palace and therefore have the greatest impact on the lives of the occupants.

Look out for the Annual and Monthly stars number 2, 5 and 9 in all 9 palaces and cure them.

Following the above procedure you first concentrate on the main palaces. Thereafter you take care of the stars number 2, 5 and 9 in any of the 9 palaces. Having done that the building will contain energies, which support well-being and positive developments.

If you aim at more, you may apply any of the water formulas and try to harmonize the energies of the Earth Base, the Facing, the Mountain, the Annual, the Monthly and the stars of the Later Heaven arrangement by working out their Host/Guest relationships in the system of the Five Elements to find the correct countermeasures and enhancers.

MAY ALL BE WELL

About The Author

Born 1934 in Berlin, the author is a qualified engineer and gemologist. He served as a German diplomat for 37 years mostly in Asian countries. Now retired, he lives in Bangkok and devotes his time to research and teaching of Feng Shui.

He acquired a fascination for Asian cultures early in life. When 15 he converted to Buddhism. While in Sri Lanka for 15 years he studied the ayurvedic system of medicine specializing in the treatment for mental diseases.

He studied acupuncture at a time, when very few in the West had any knowledge on it.

In studying and practicing acupuncture he often experienced that traditional formulas for the treatment of diseases gave some relieve, but rarely cured. Obsessed to understand why, he researched the fundamental principles of acupuncture and discovered how to apply them in order to cure.

Acupuncture initiated him into the Taoist Cosmology on which Feng Shui is based.

He says: understanding the energies of nature, which govern our fate and well-being is his passion in life.

Printed in Great Britain
by Amazon

43172707R00123